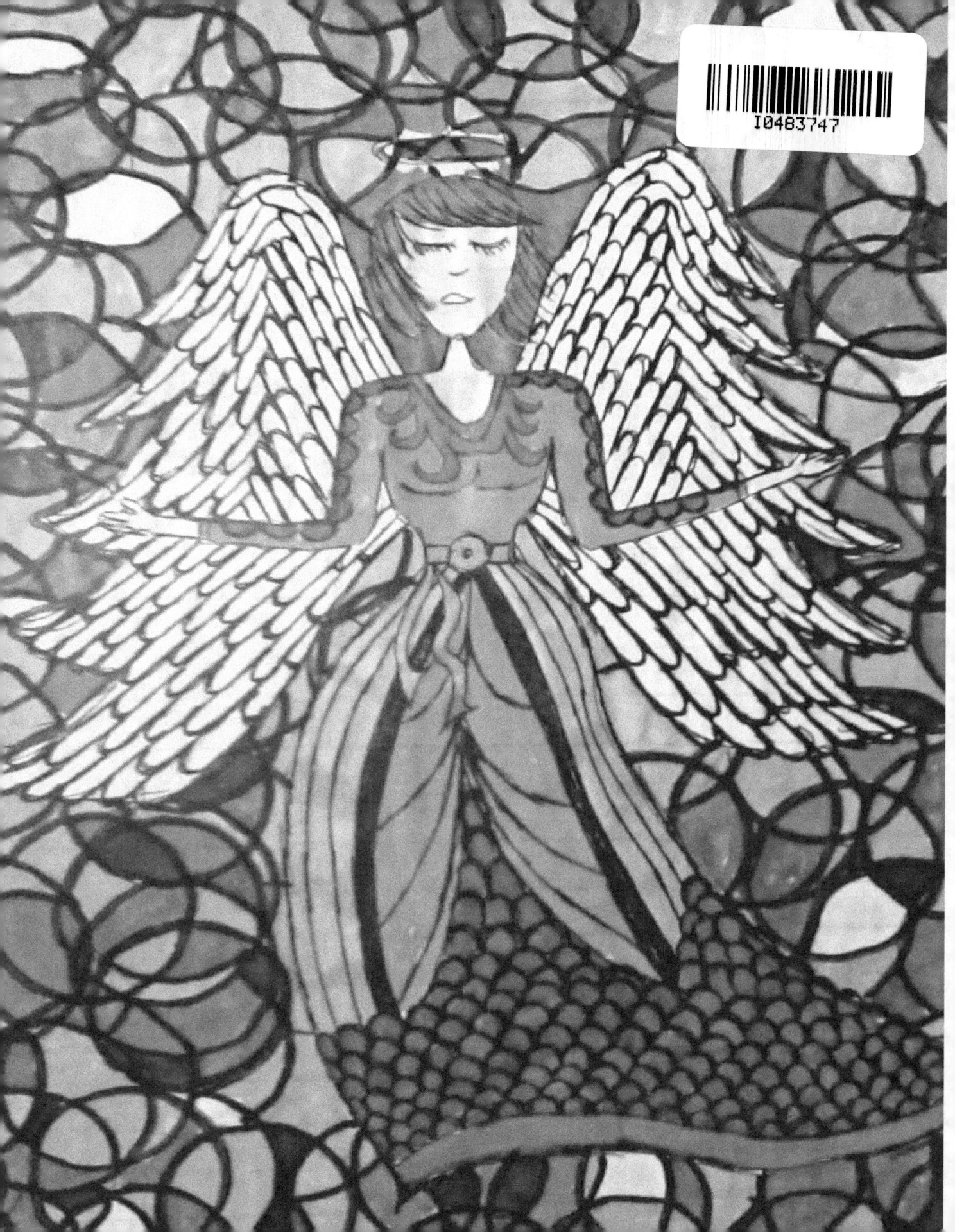

An M. Hills:

DOODLES OF FUN!

Dedication:

I want to Thank my dear friends Sherry & Paul for their insistent encouragement of my creating a coloring book from my drawings!

I want to Thank my momma, my church, God, for all their love & support.

Thank You!

A. M. Hill's:

DOODLES
OF
FUN!

Created & Illustrated By

A. M. Hill

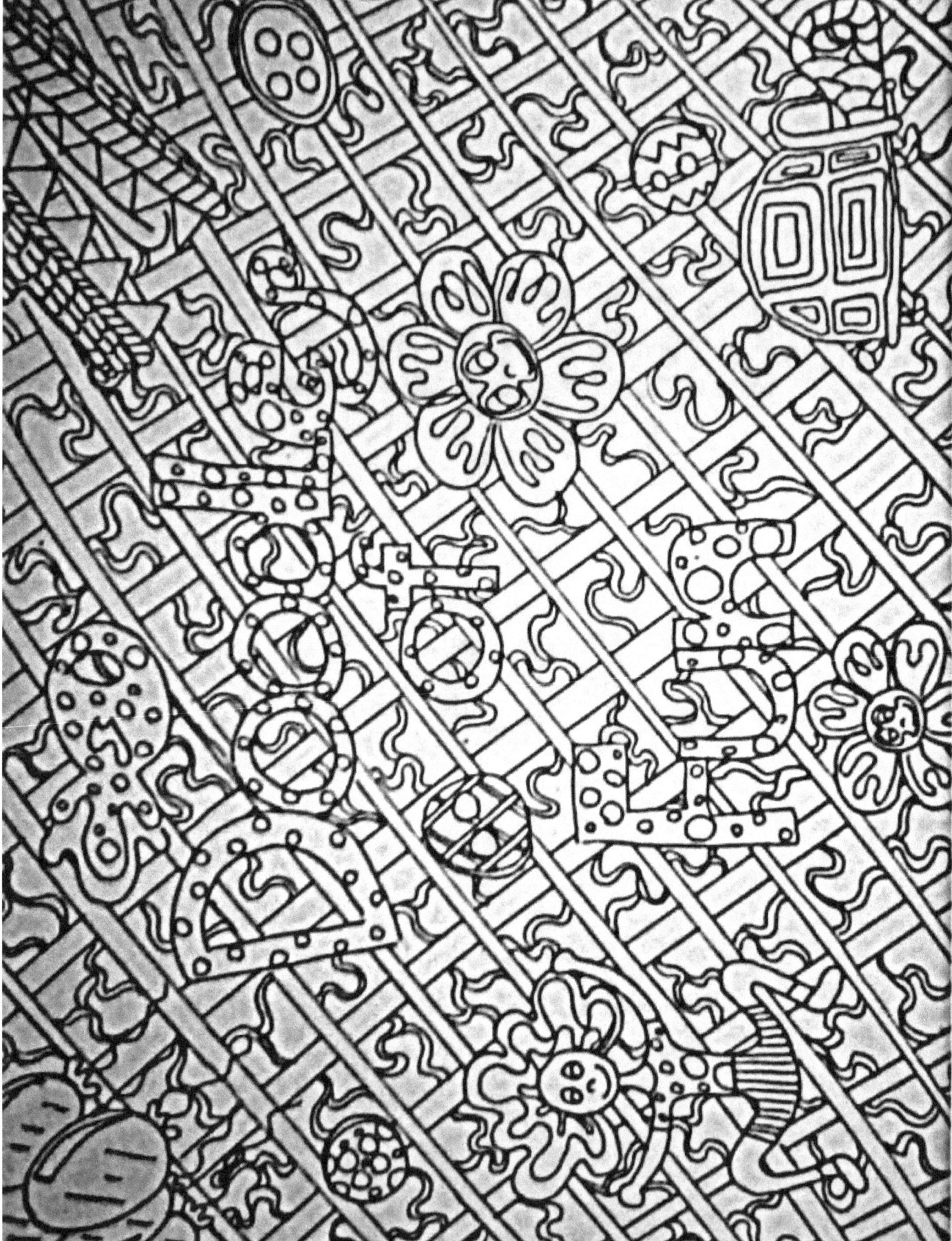

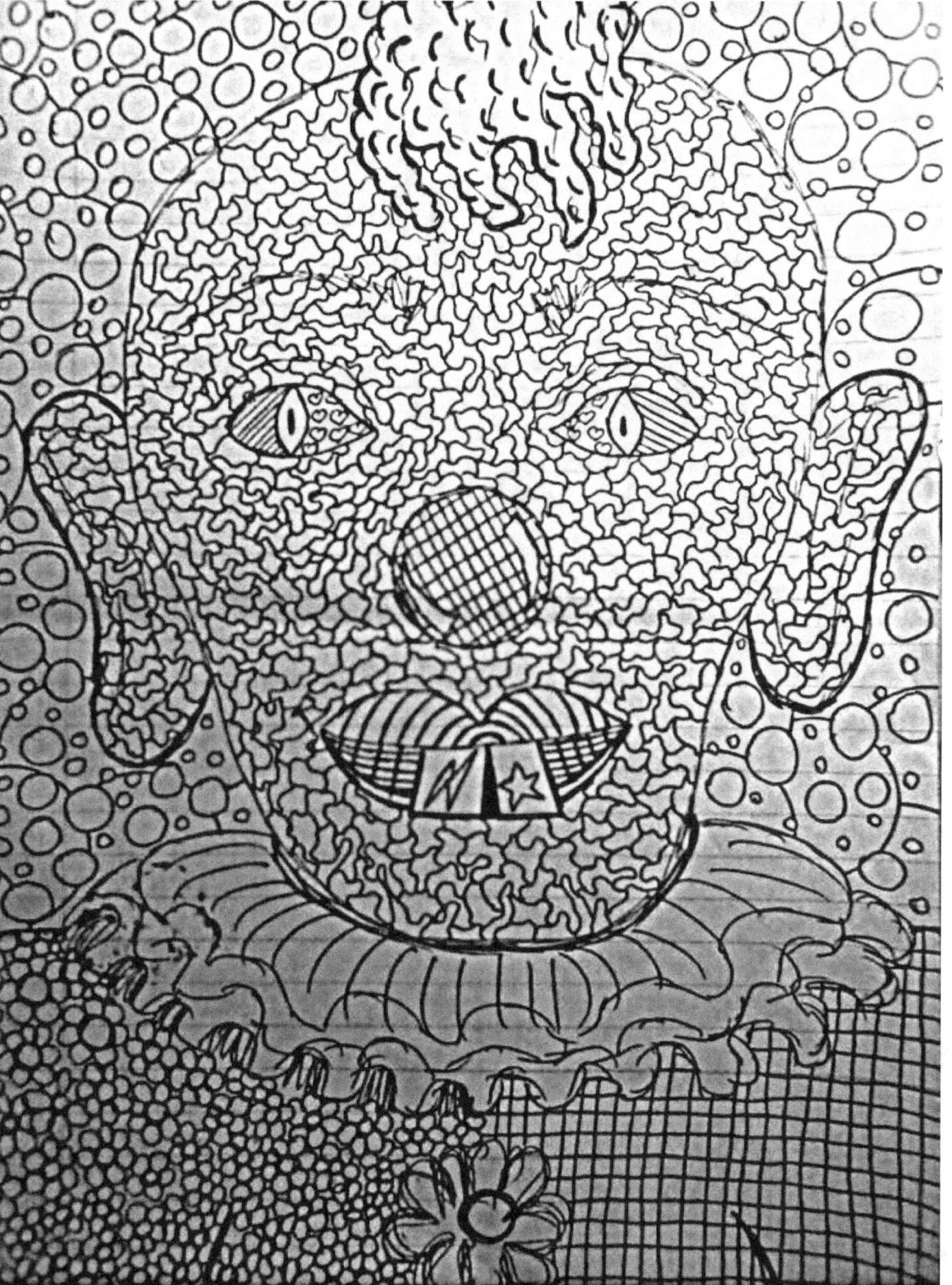

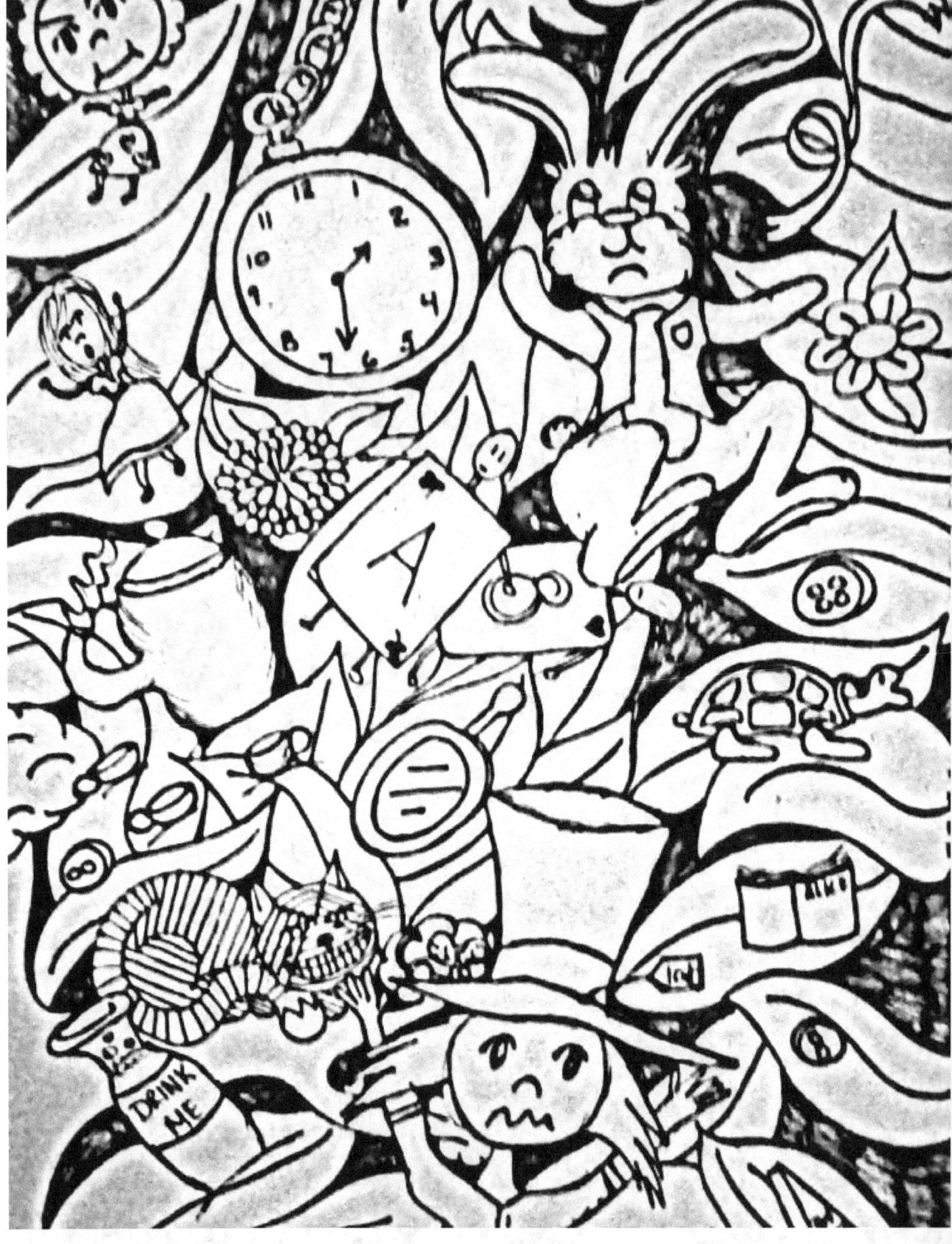

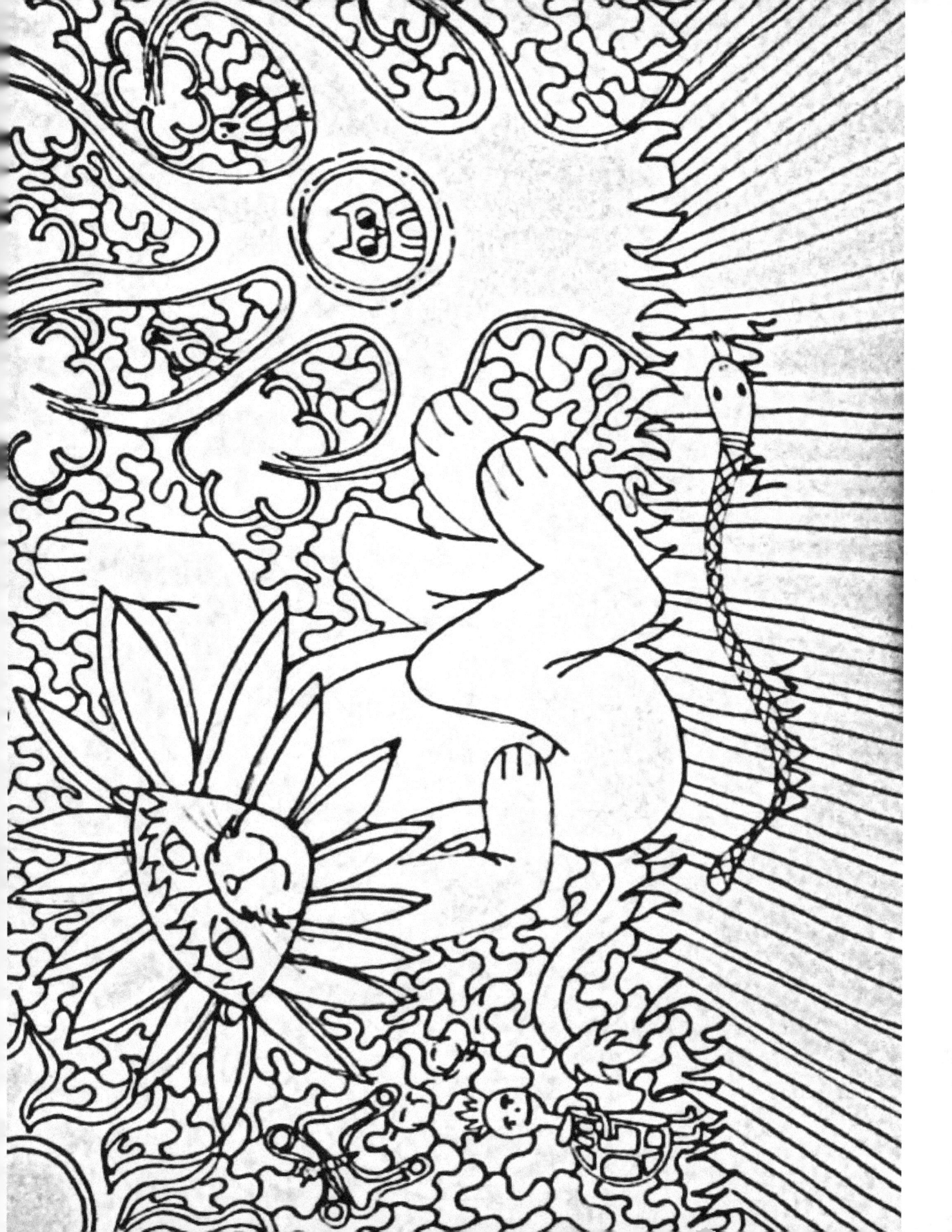

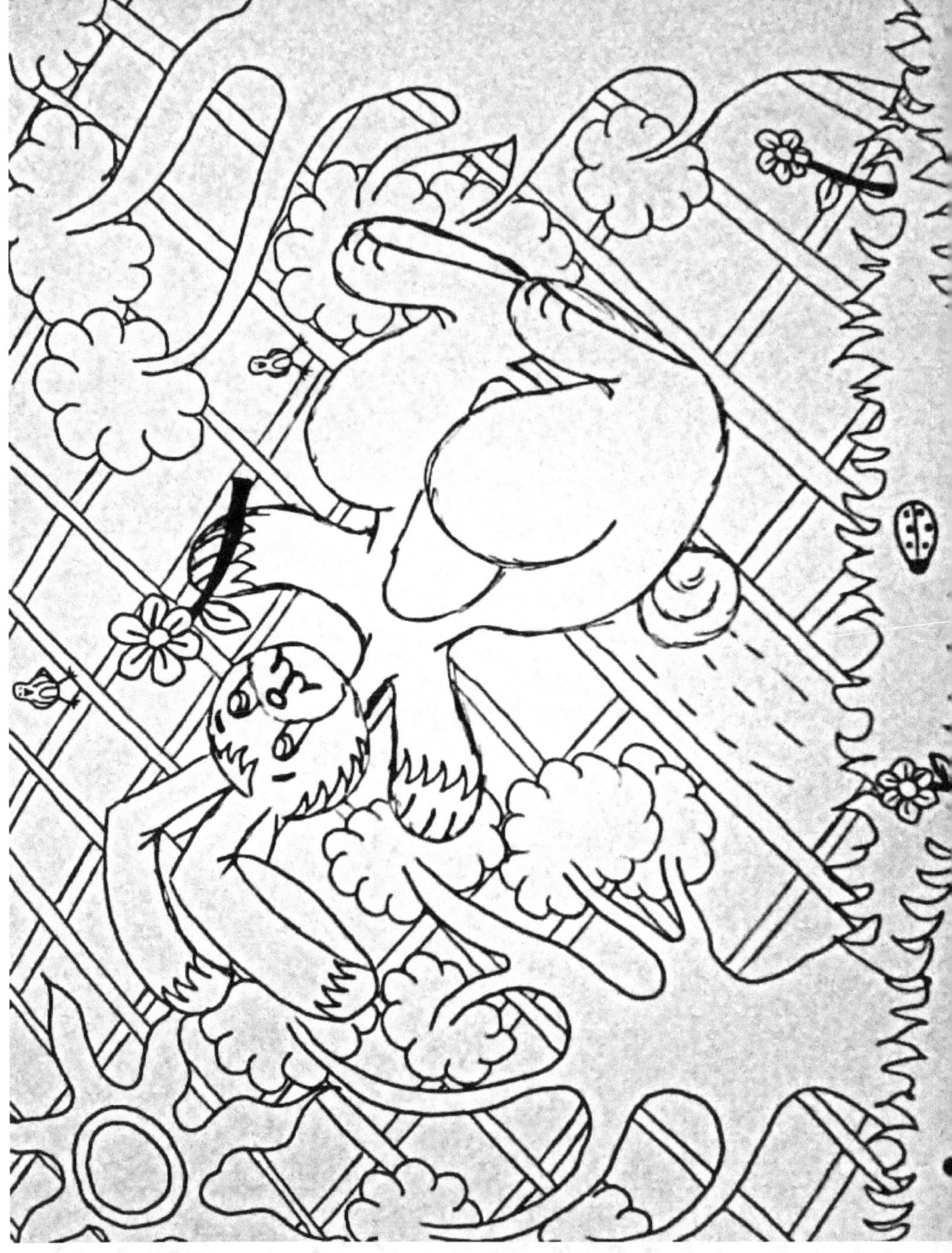

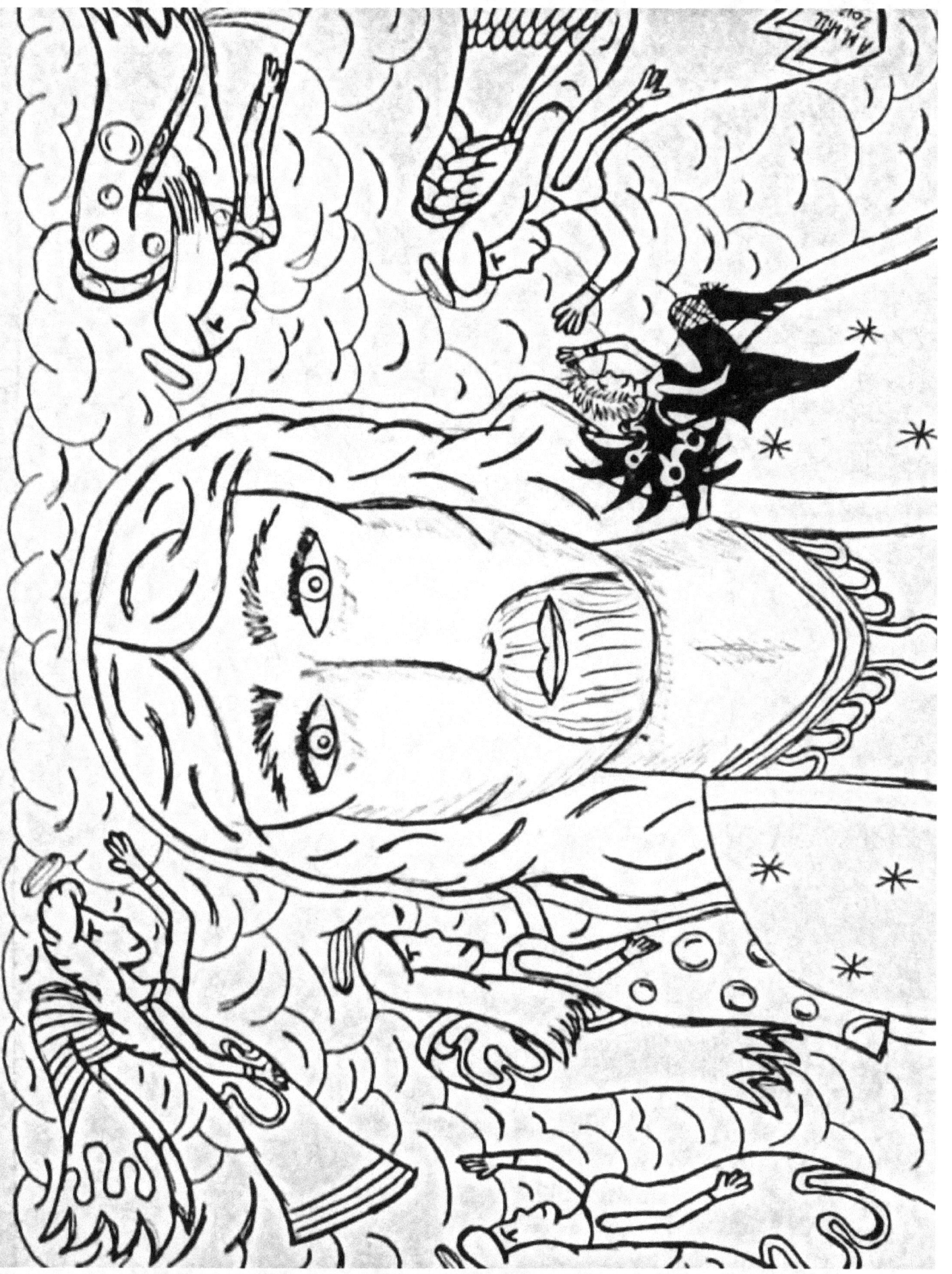

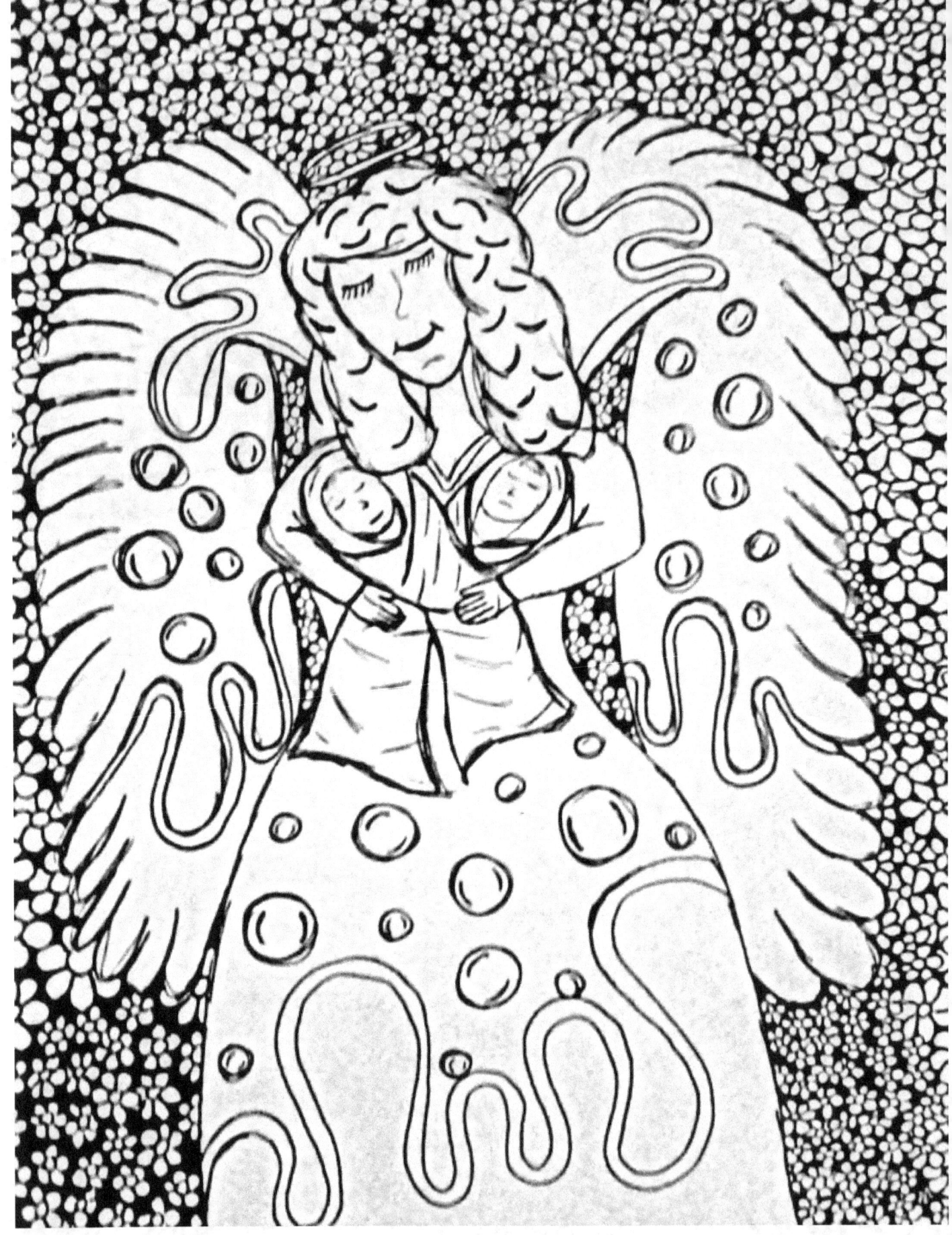

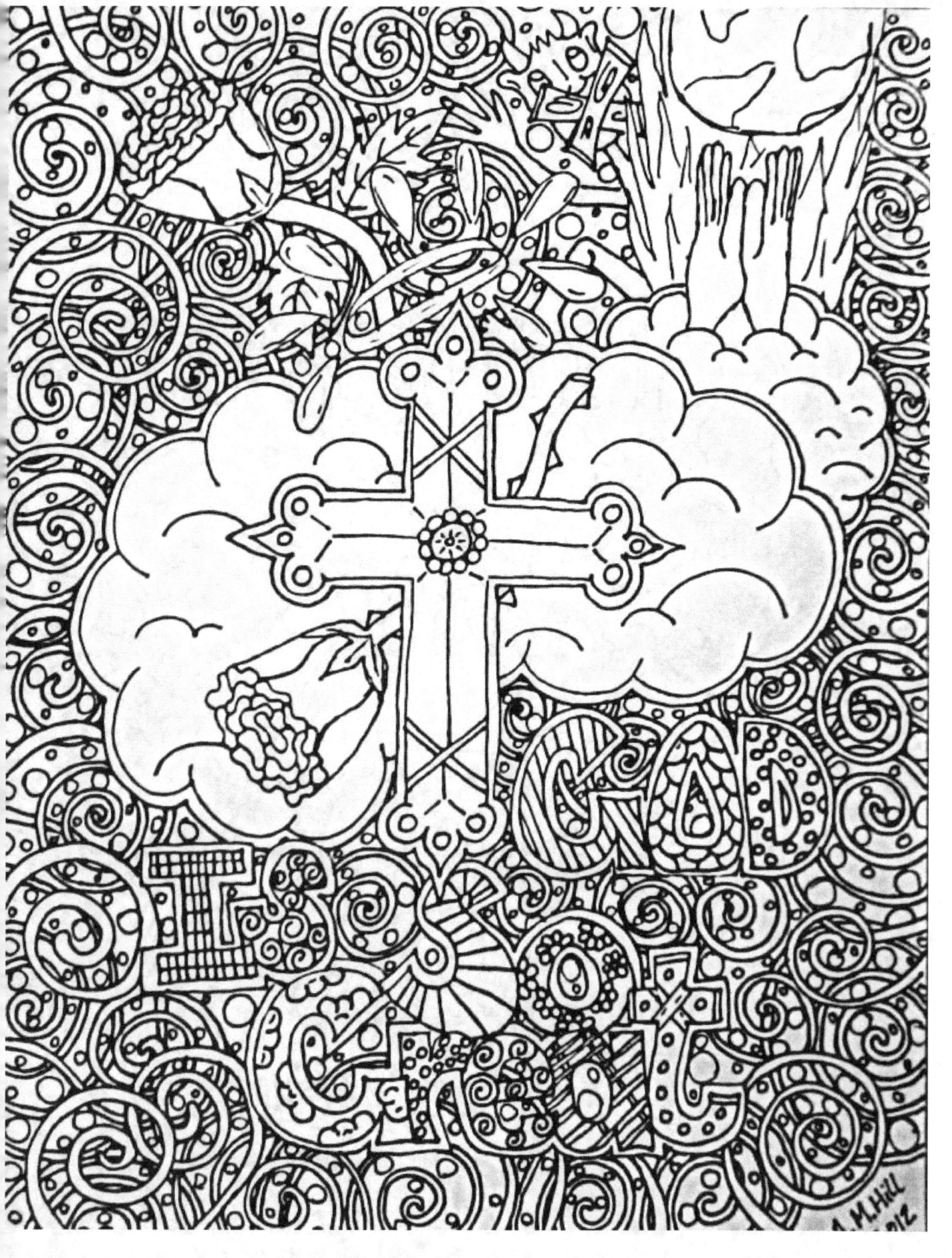

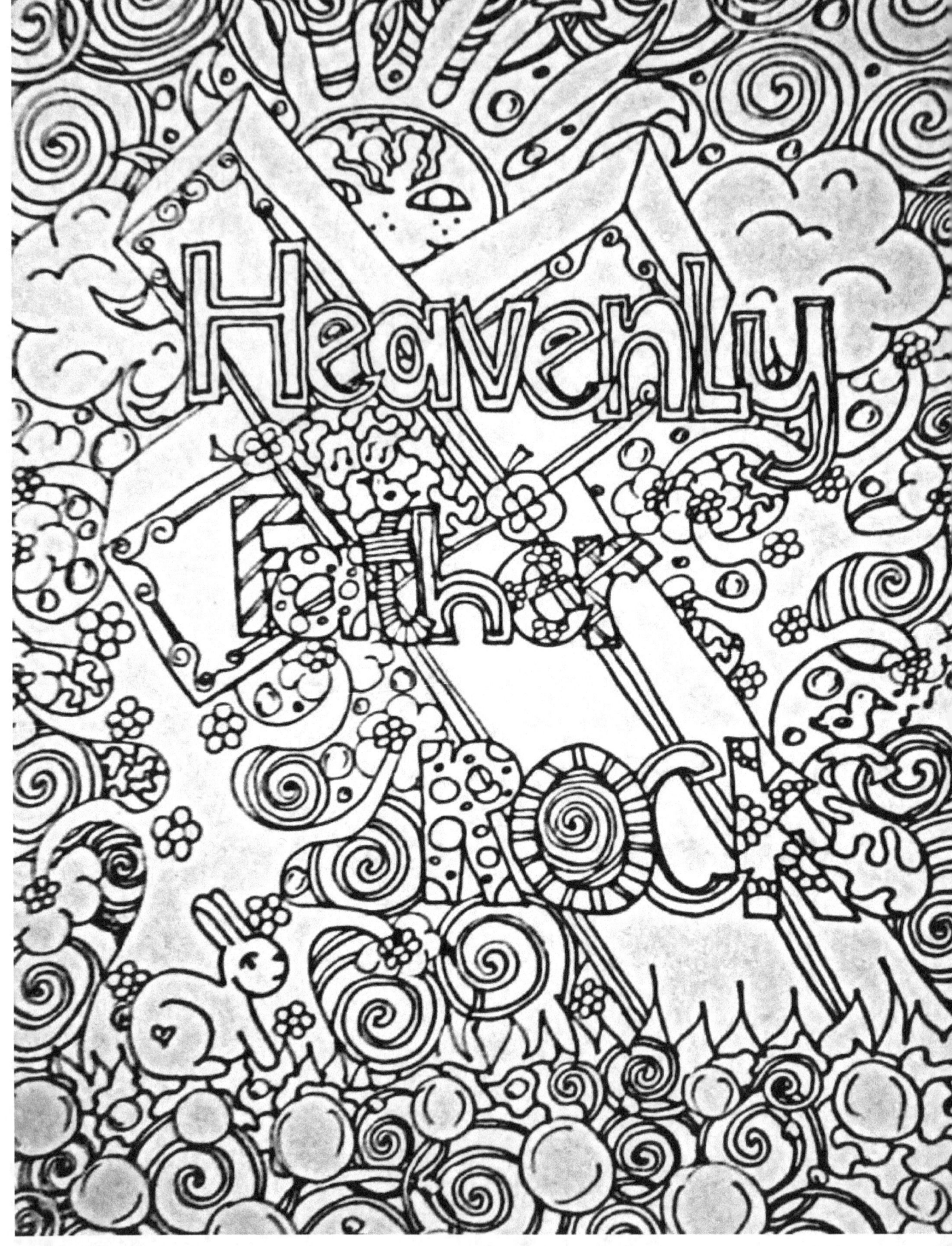

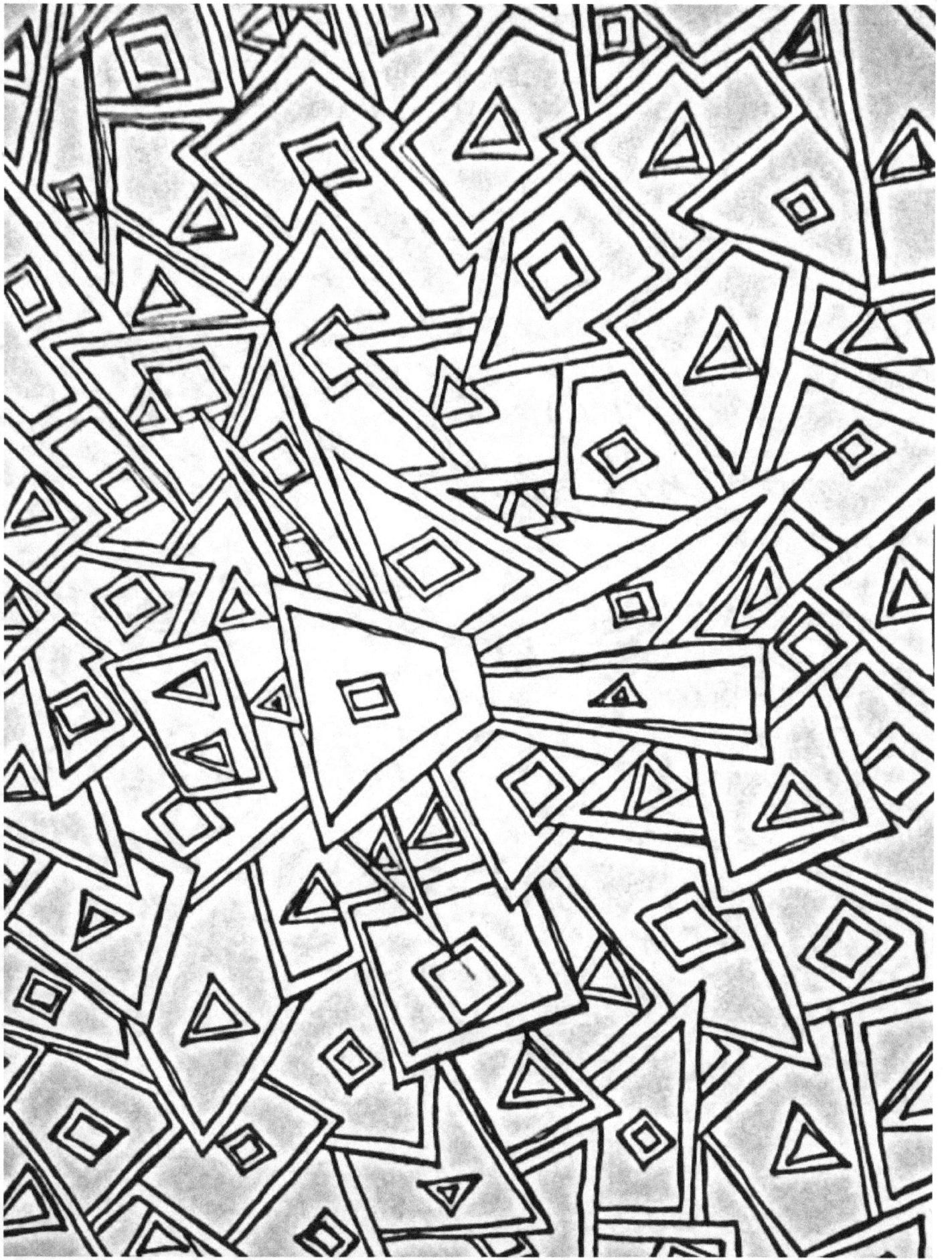

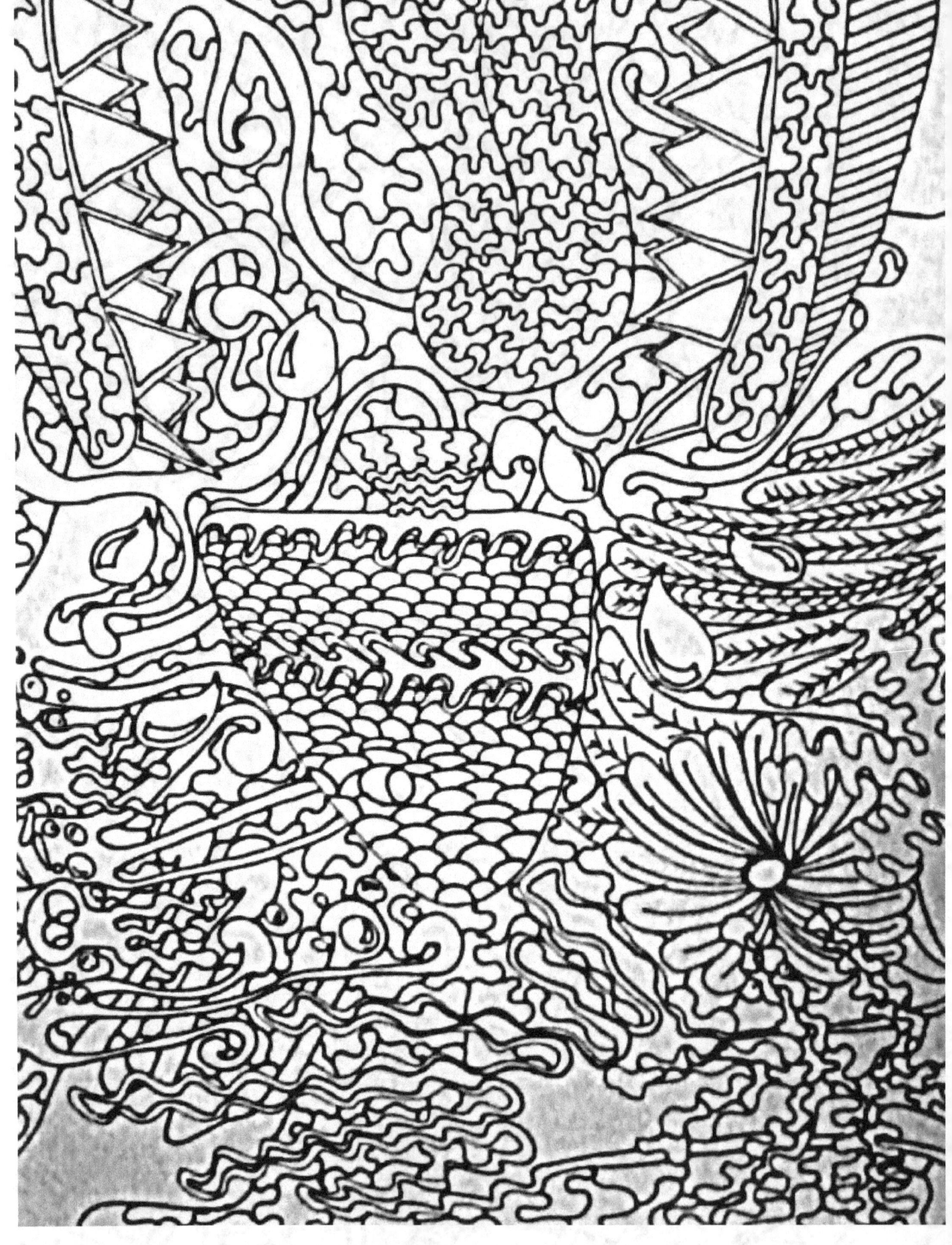

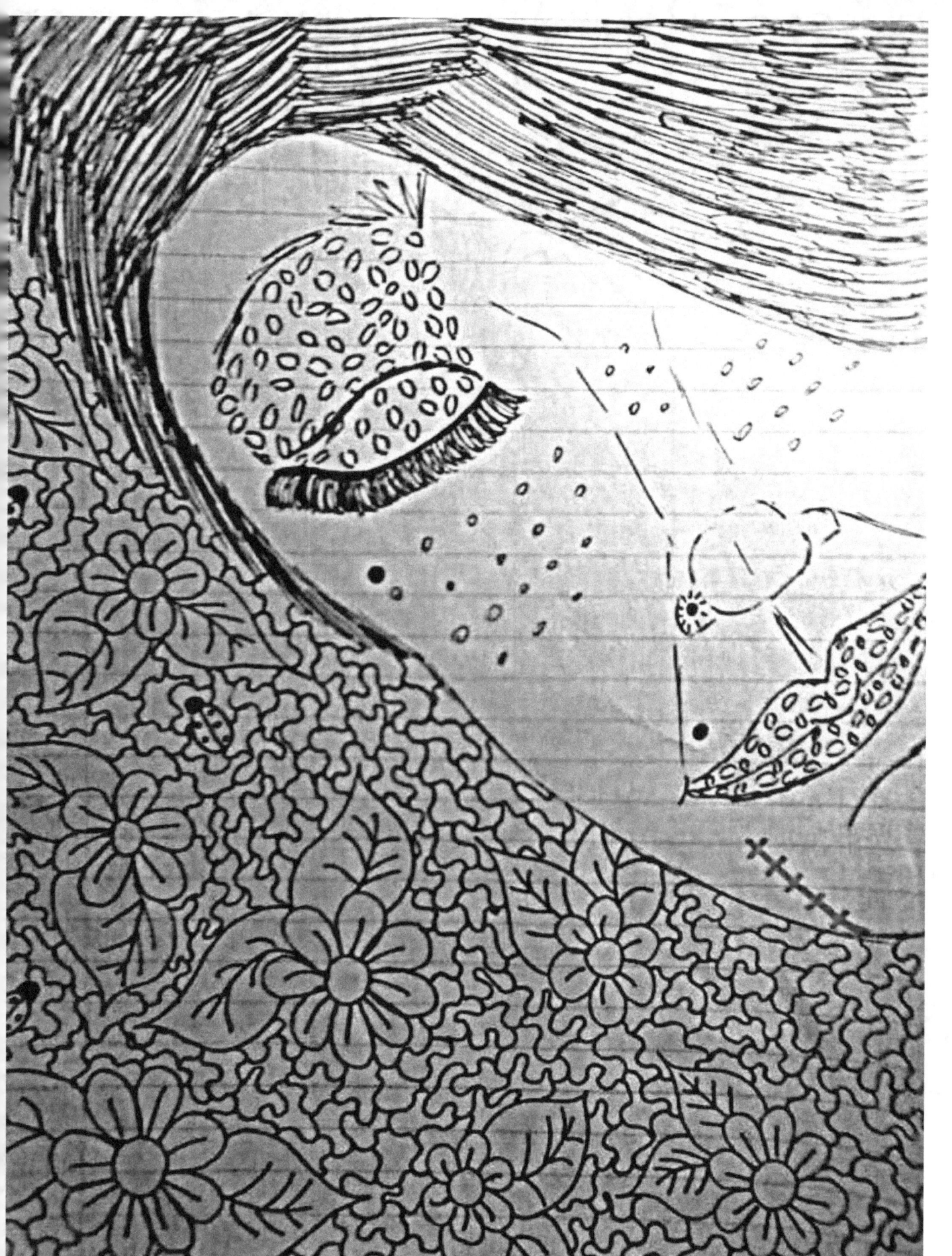

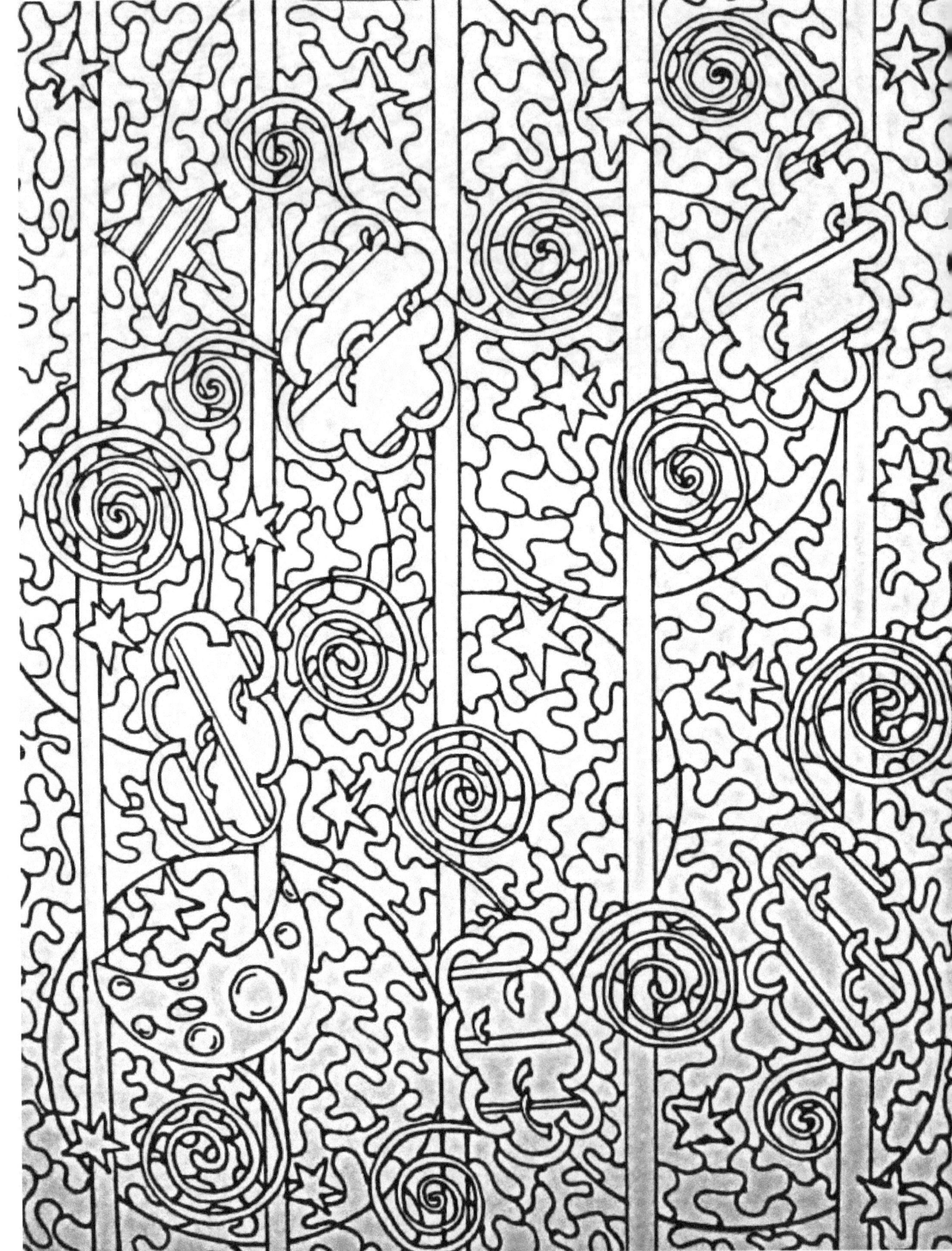

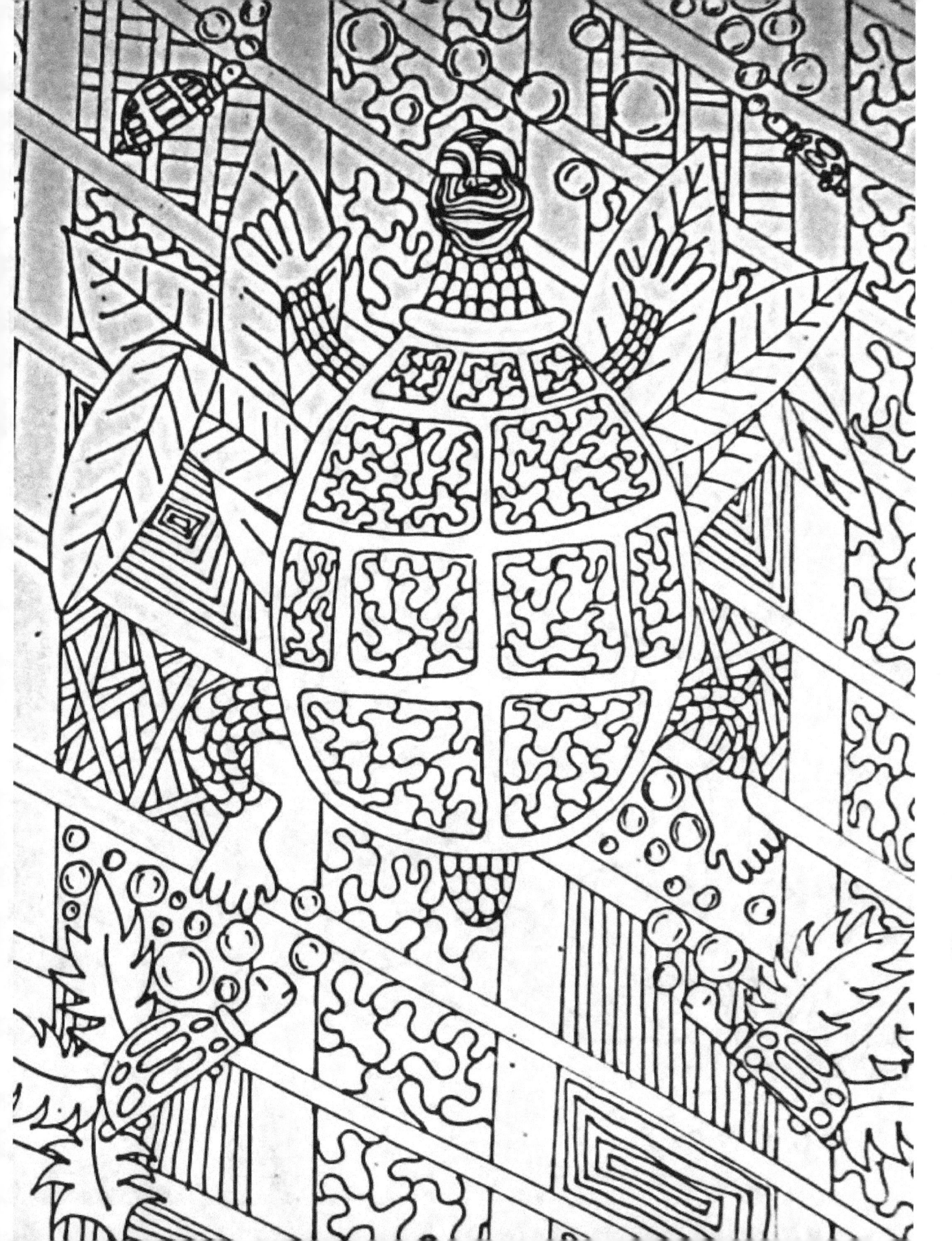

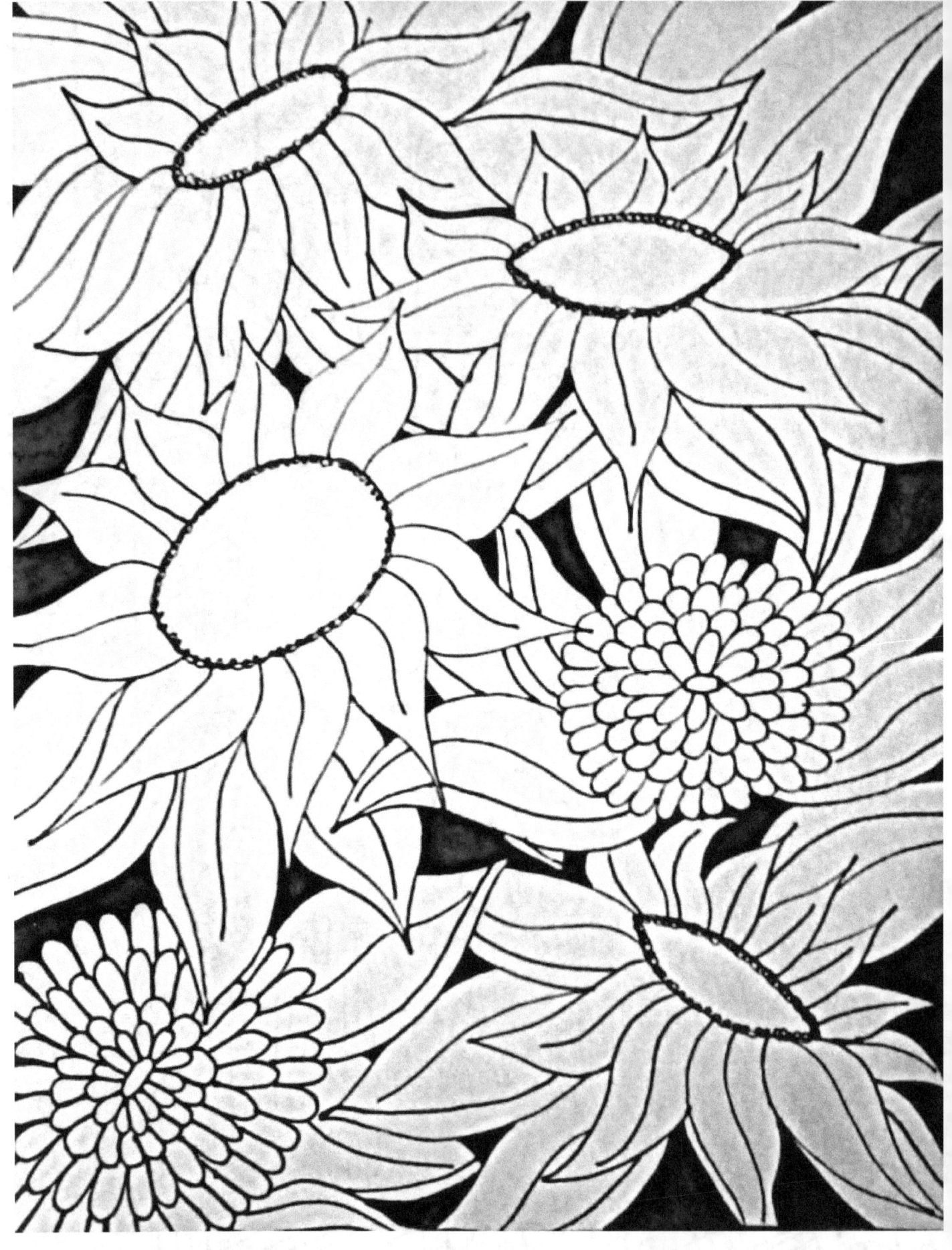

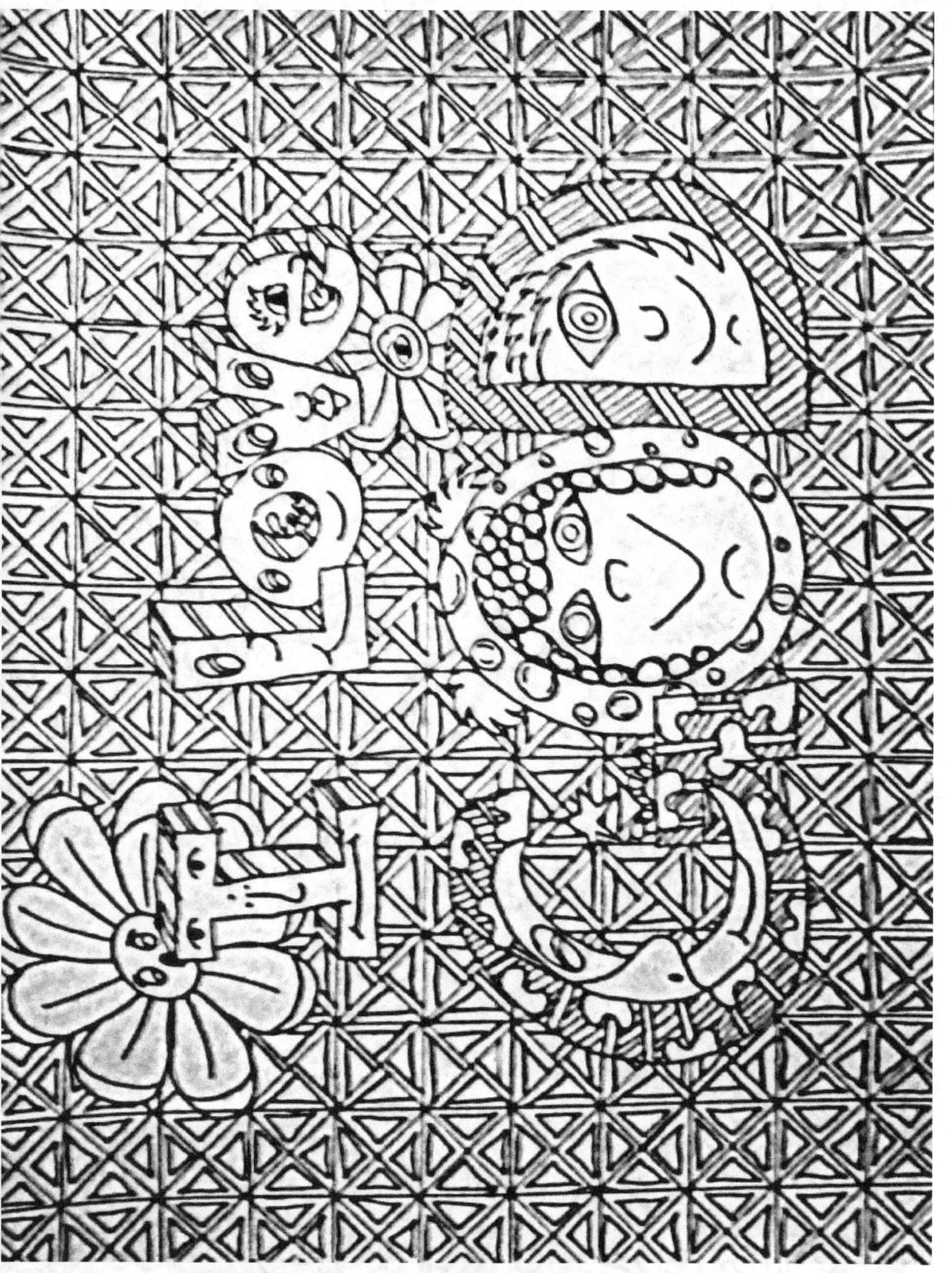

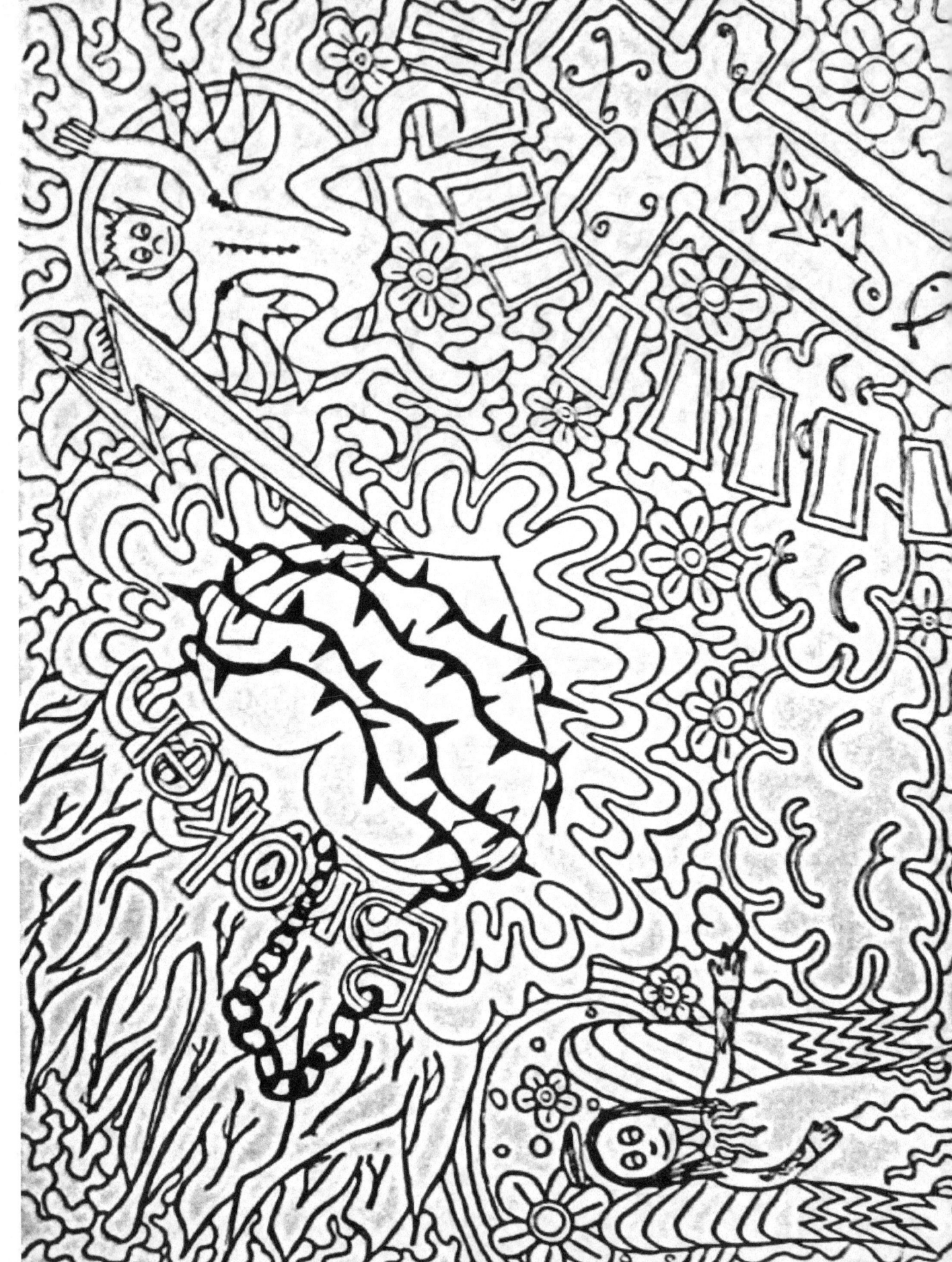

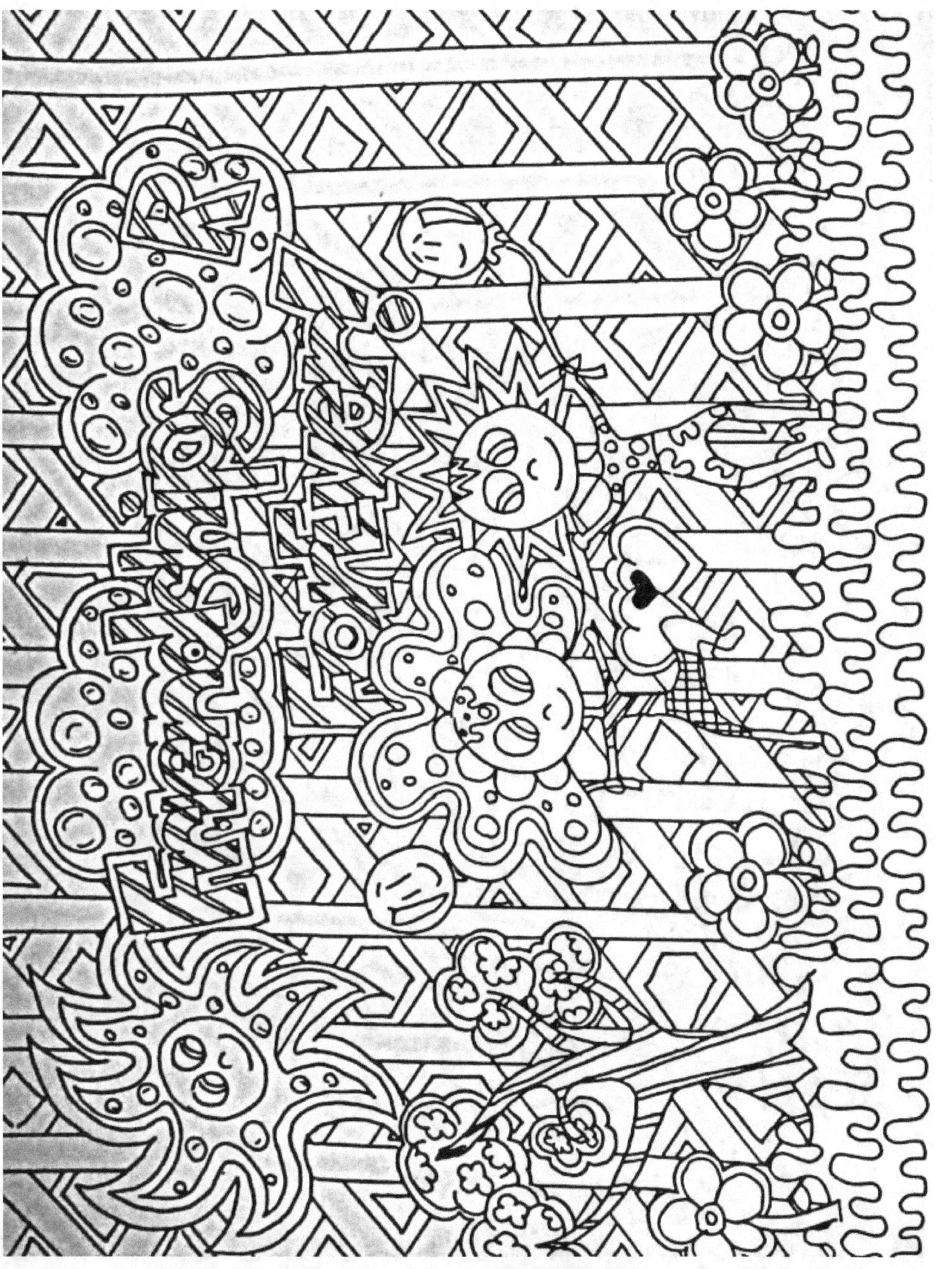

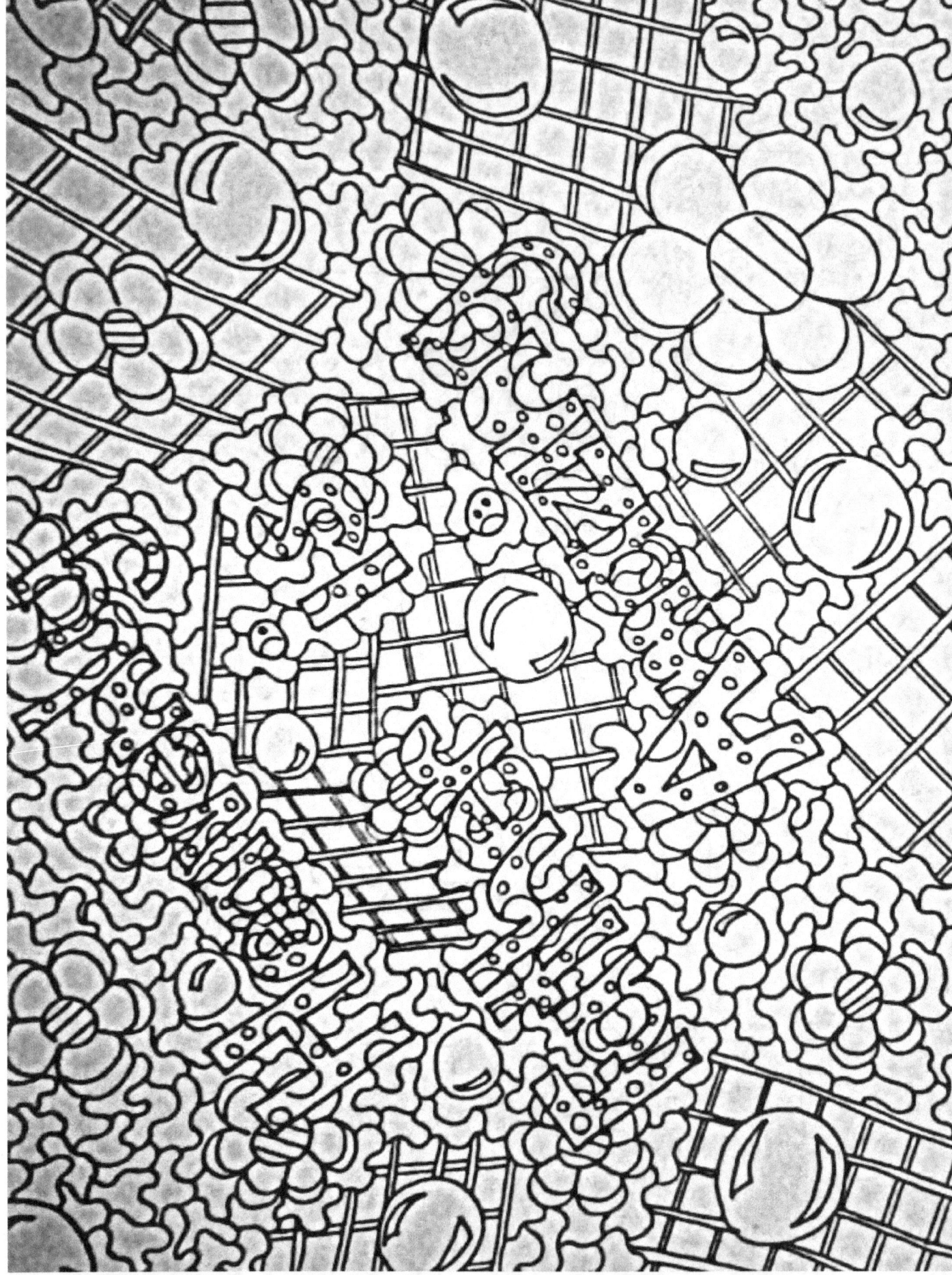

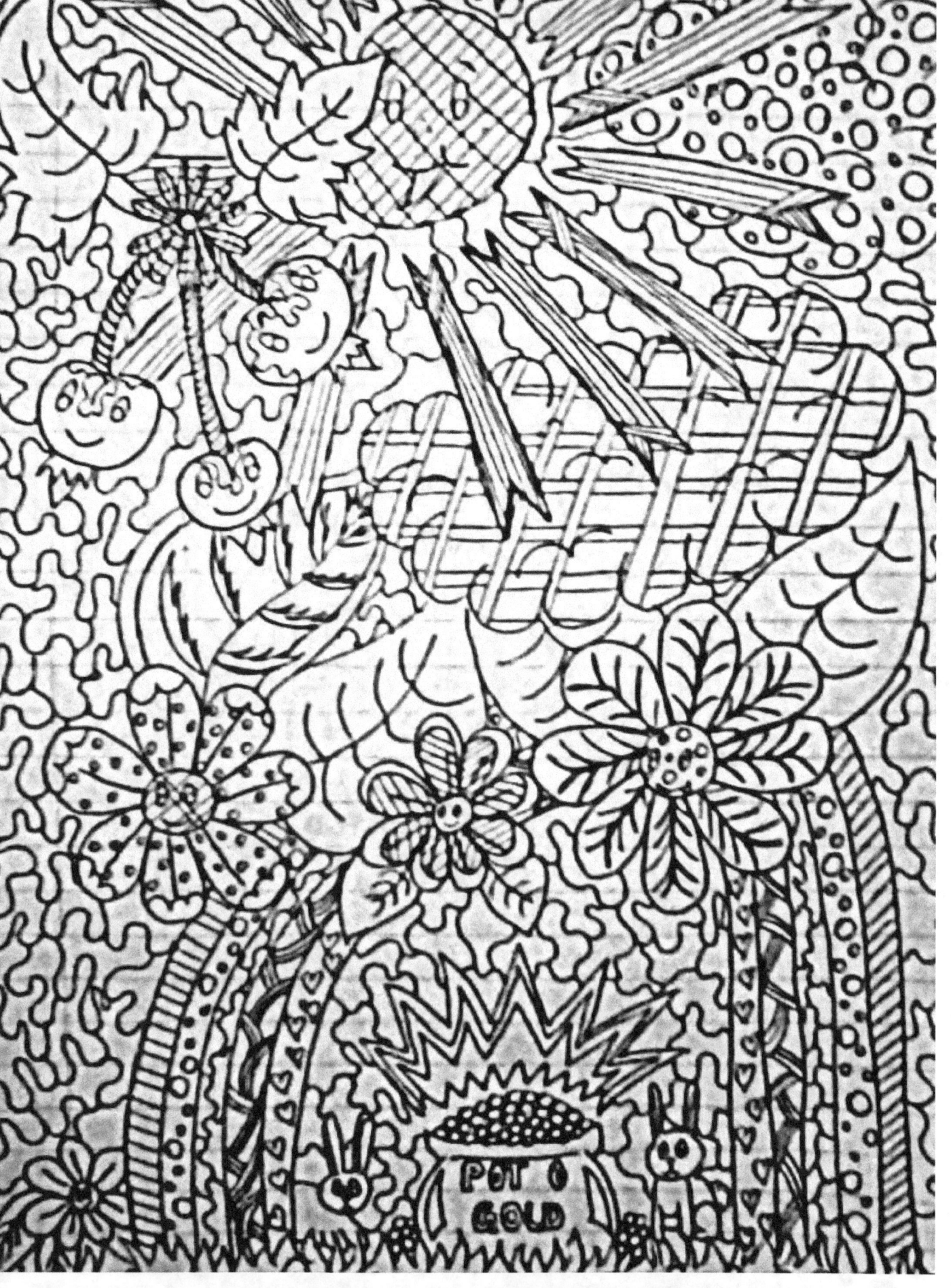

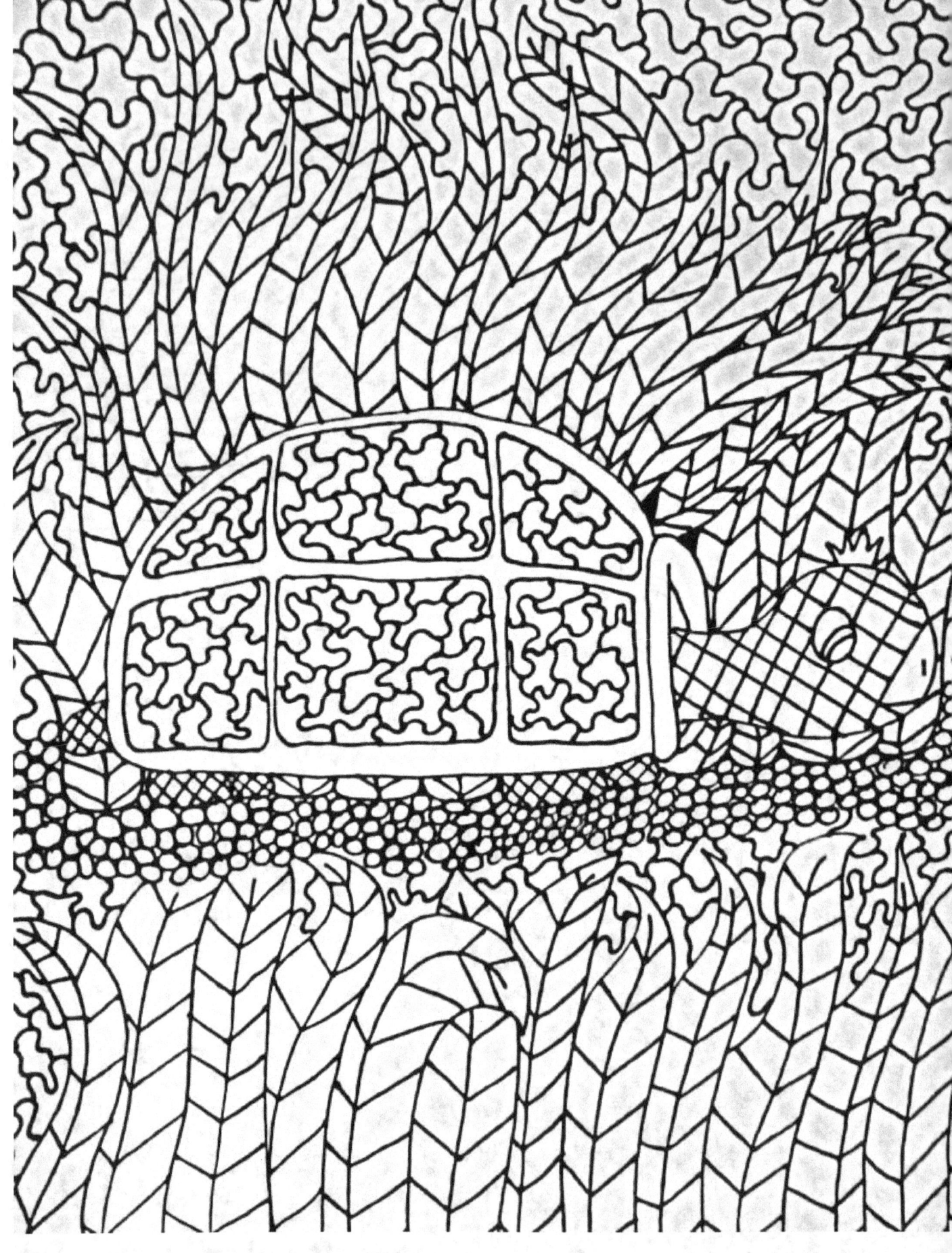

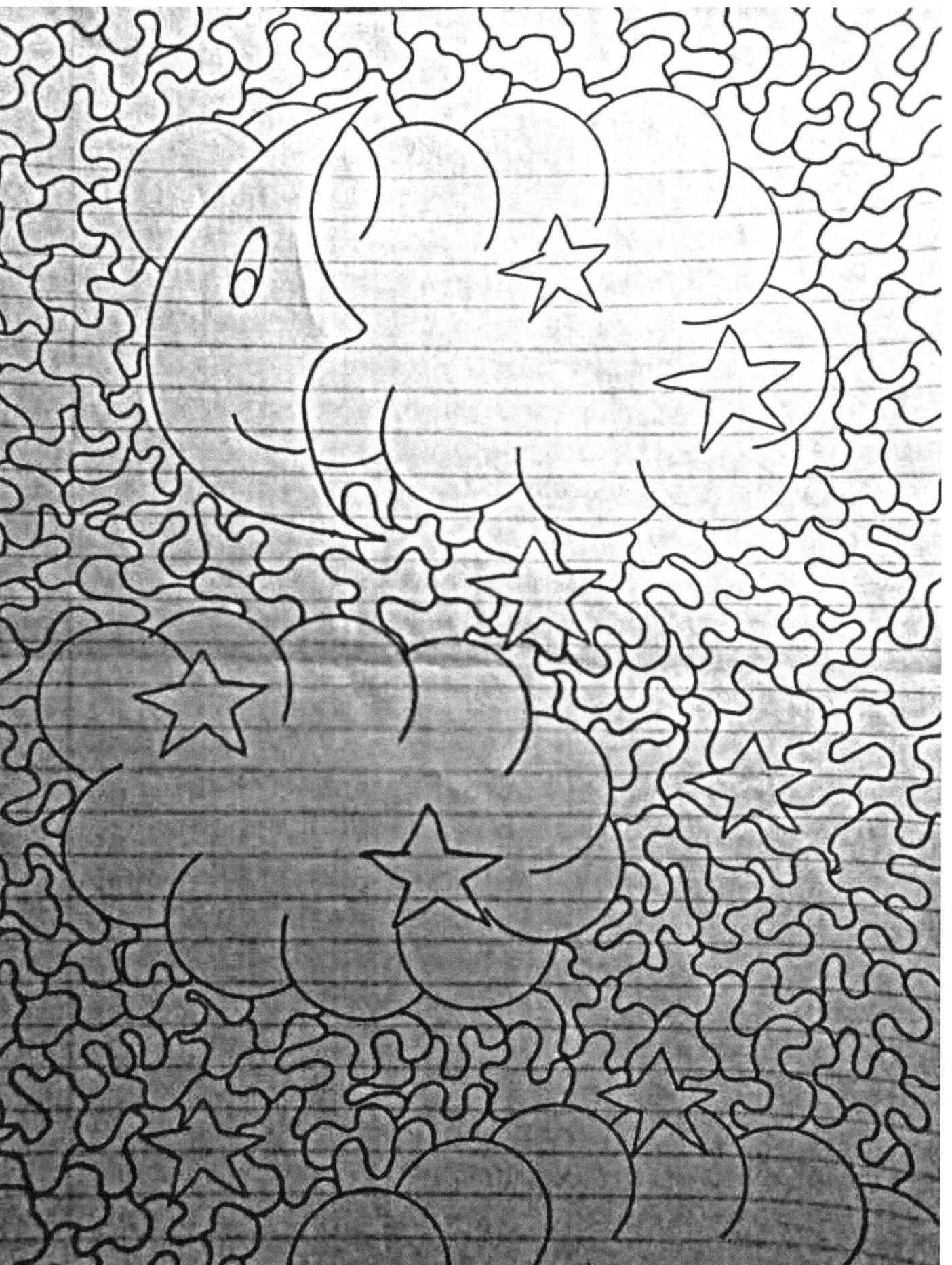

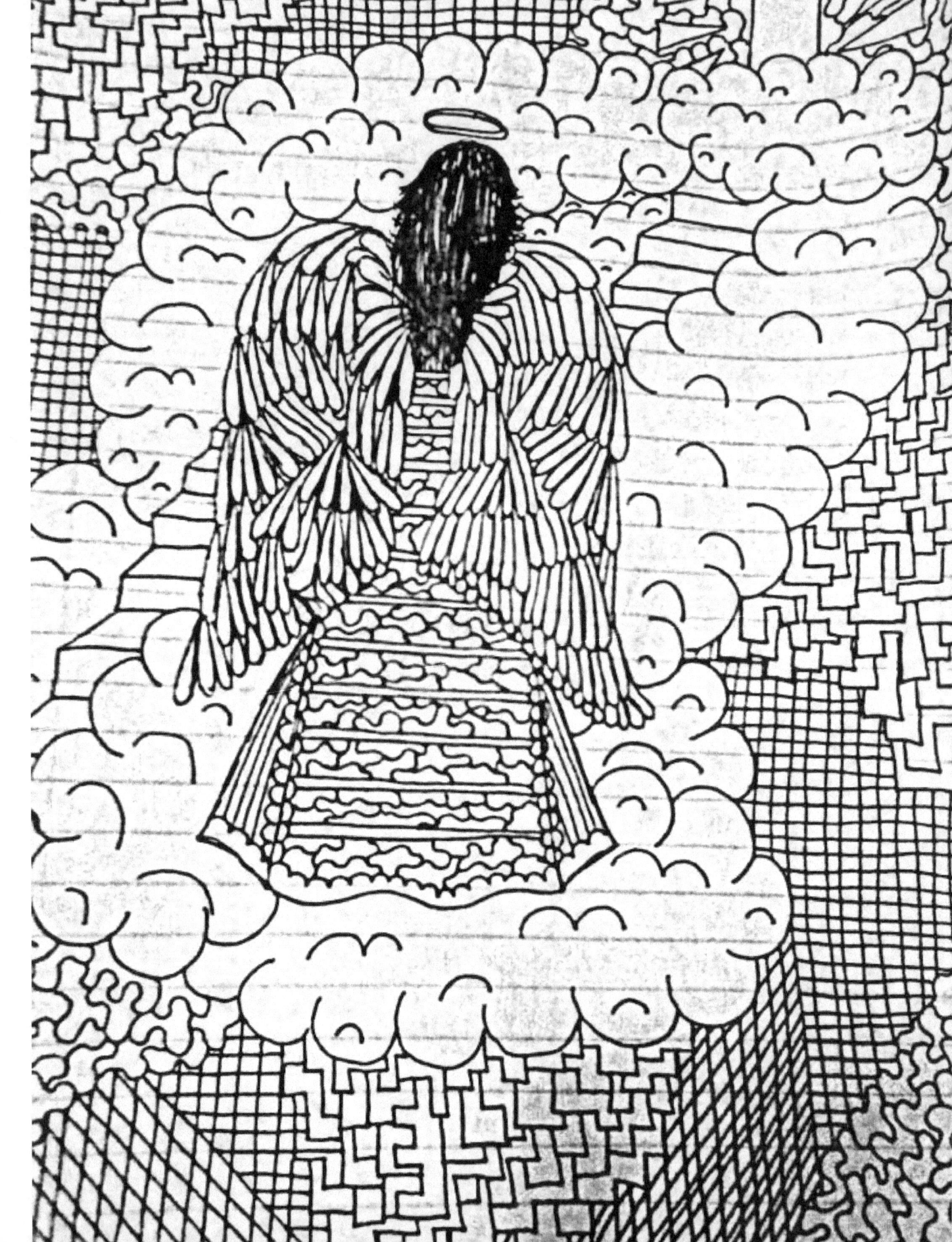

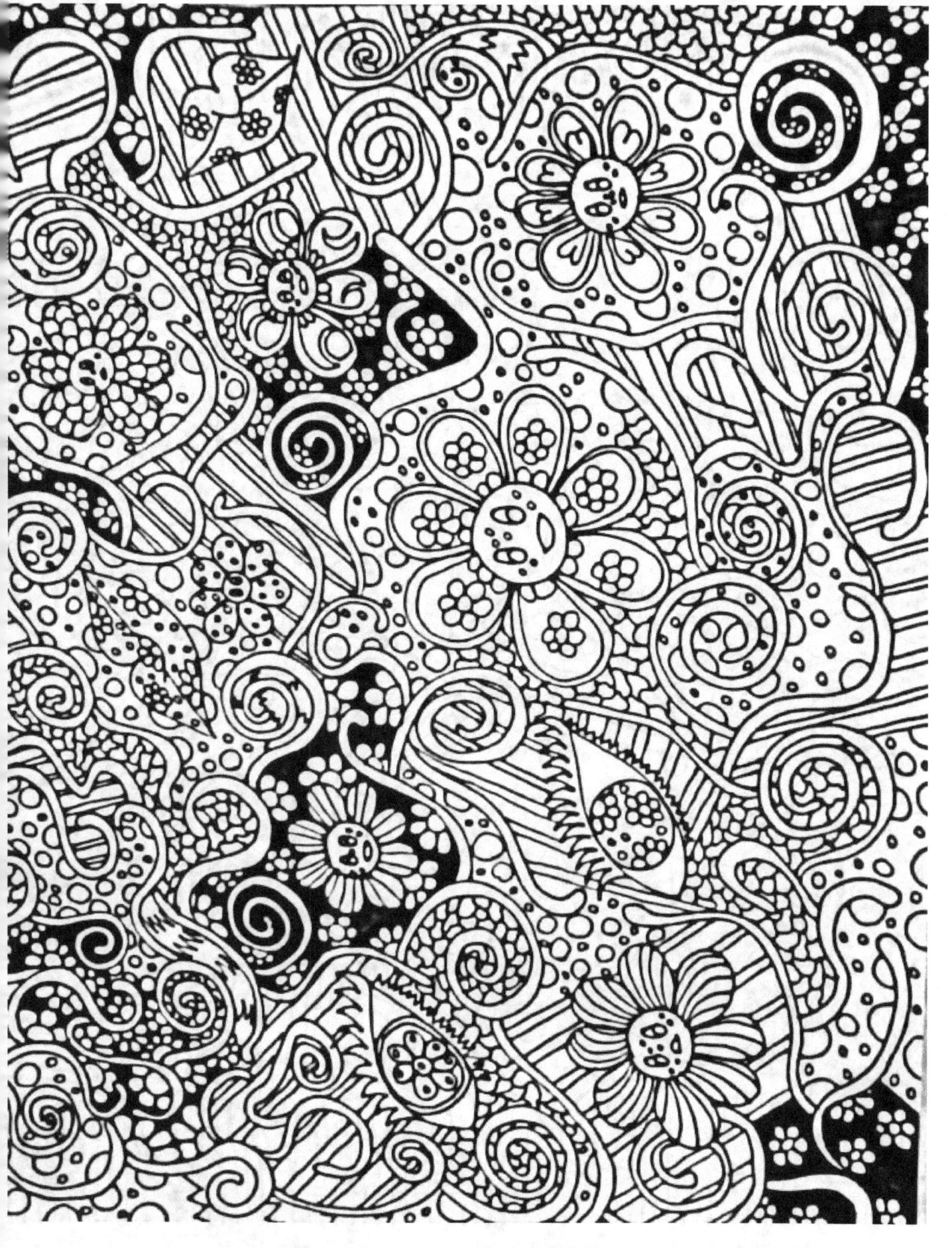

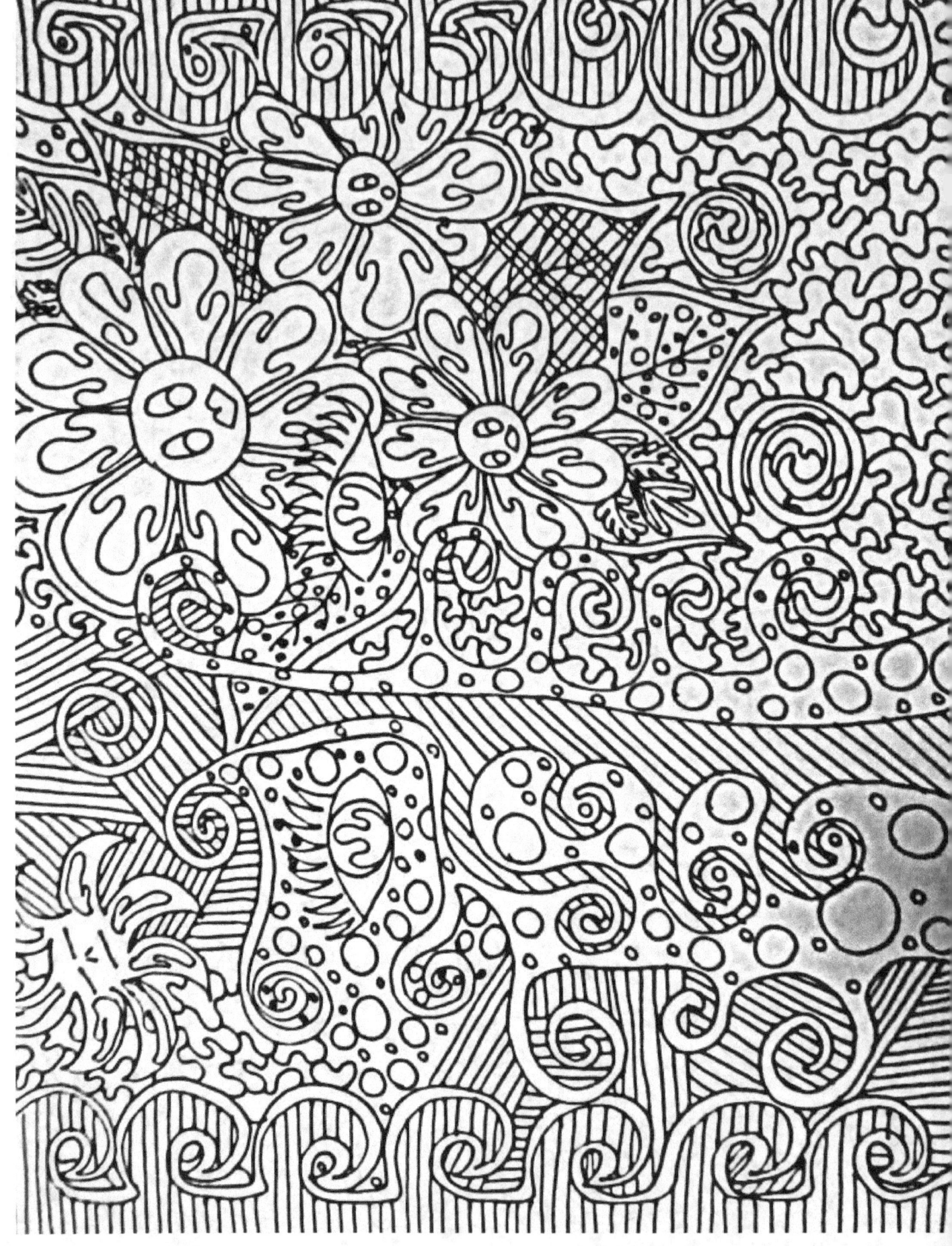

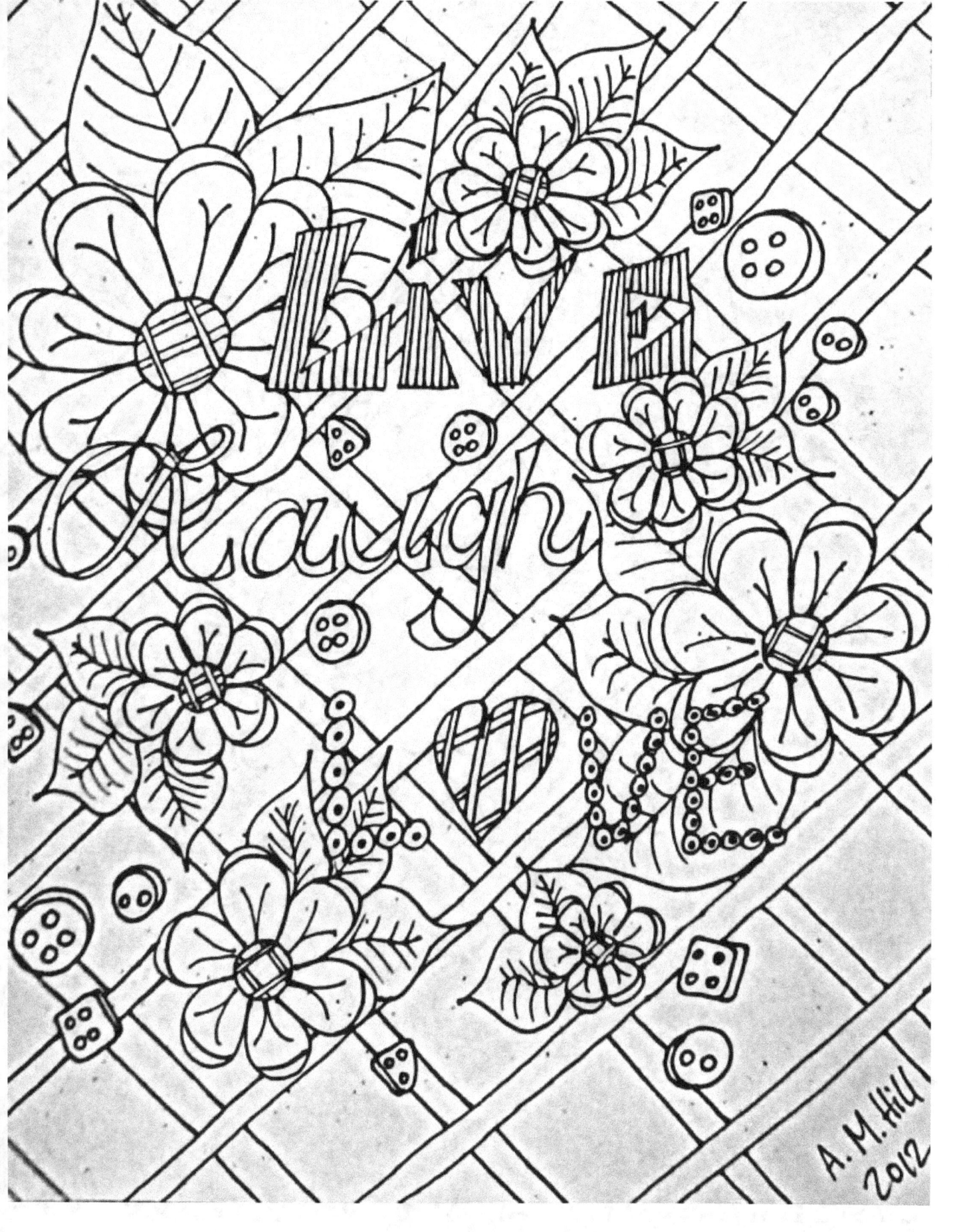

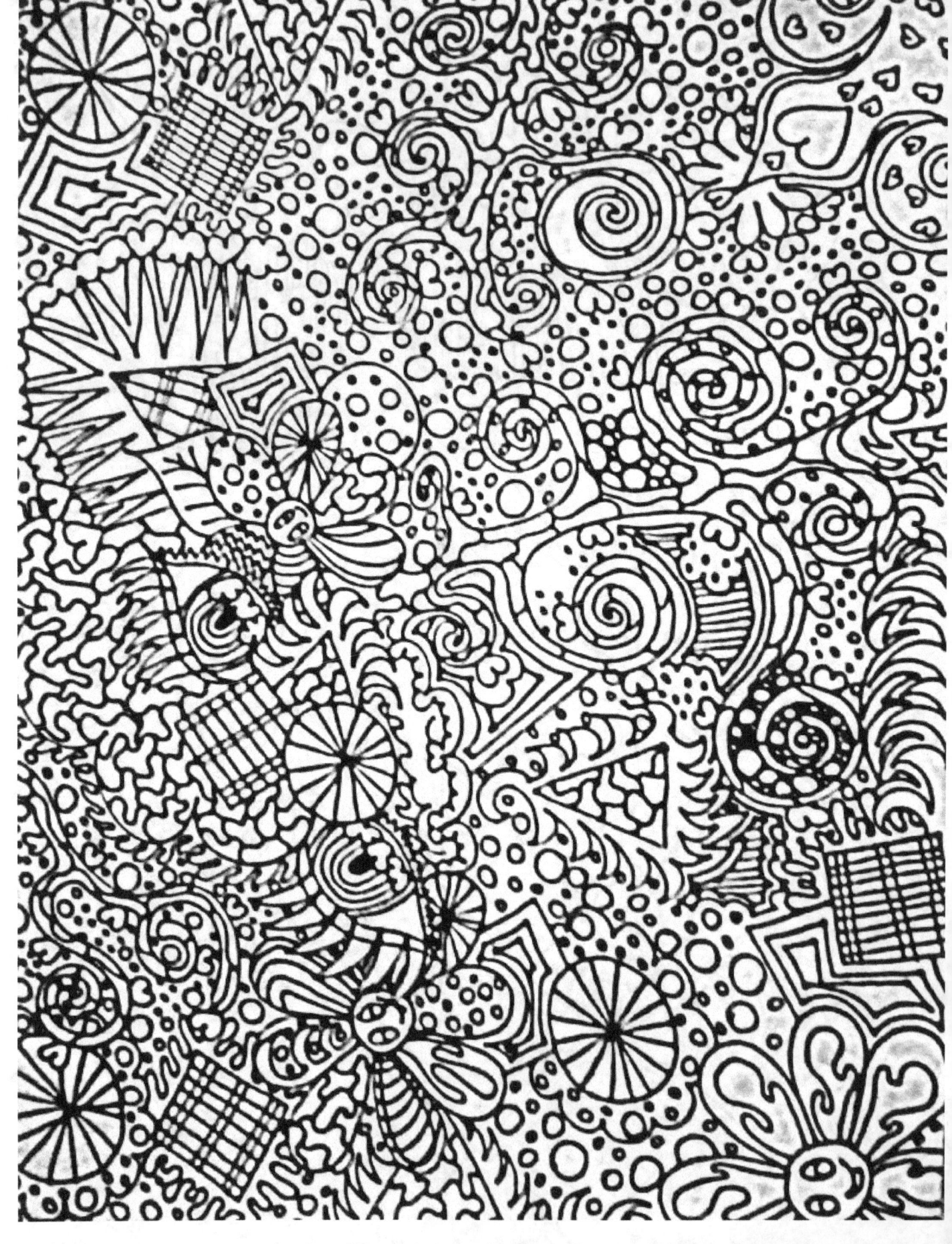

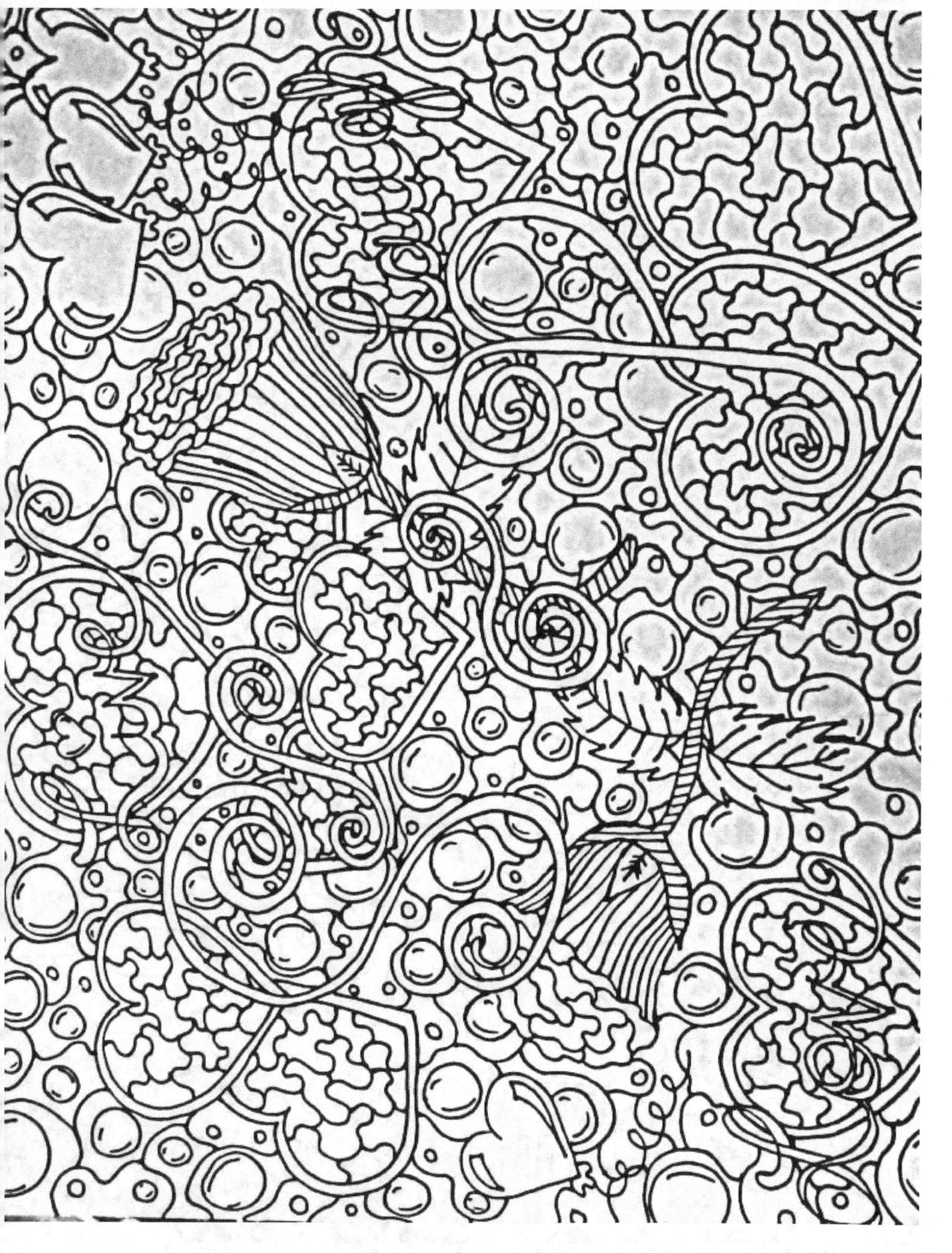

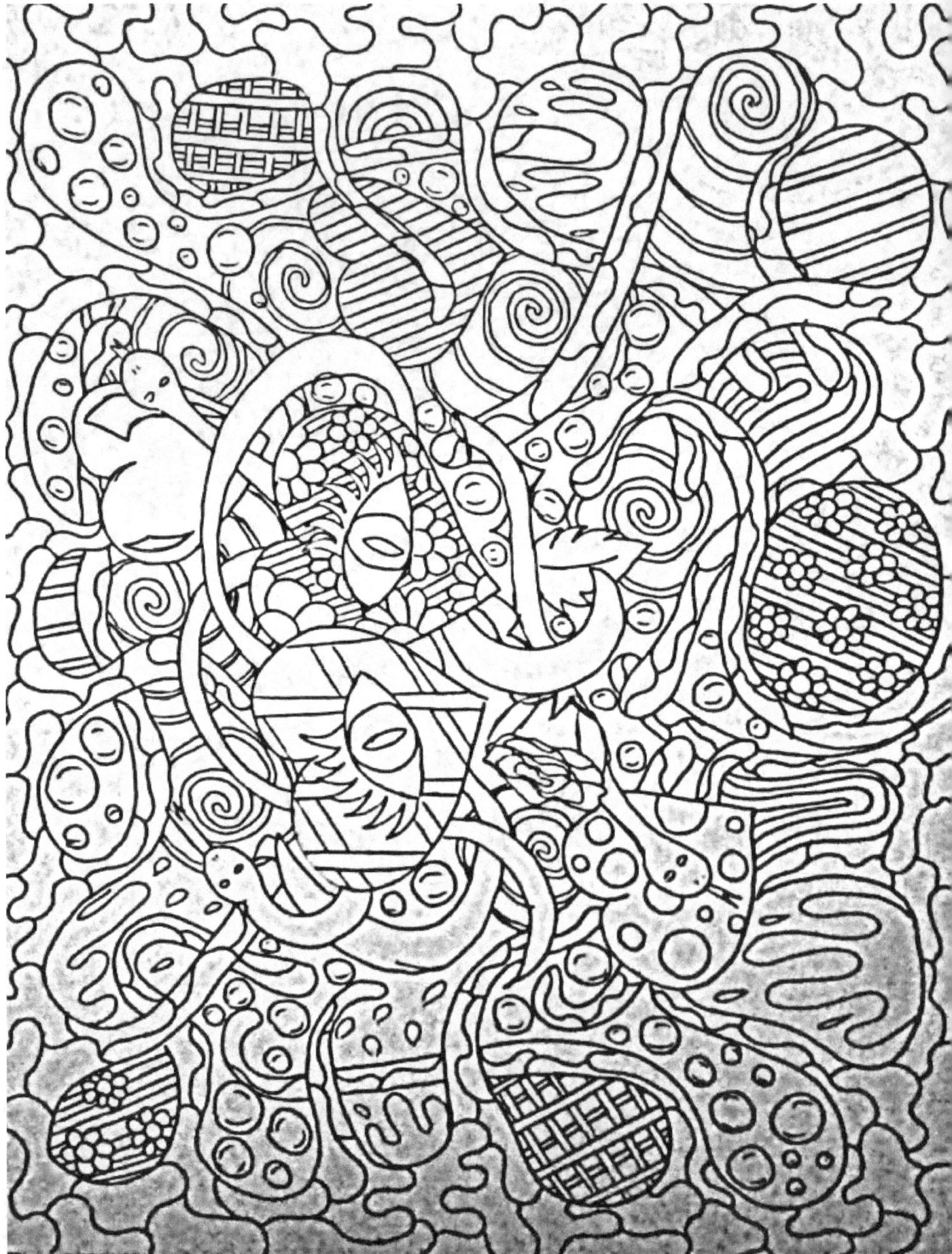

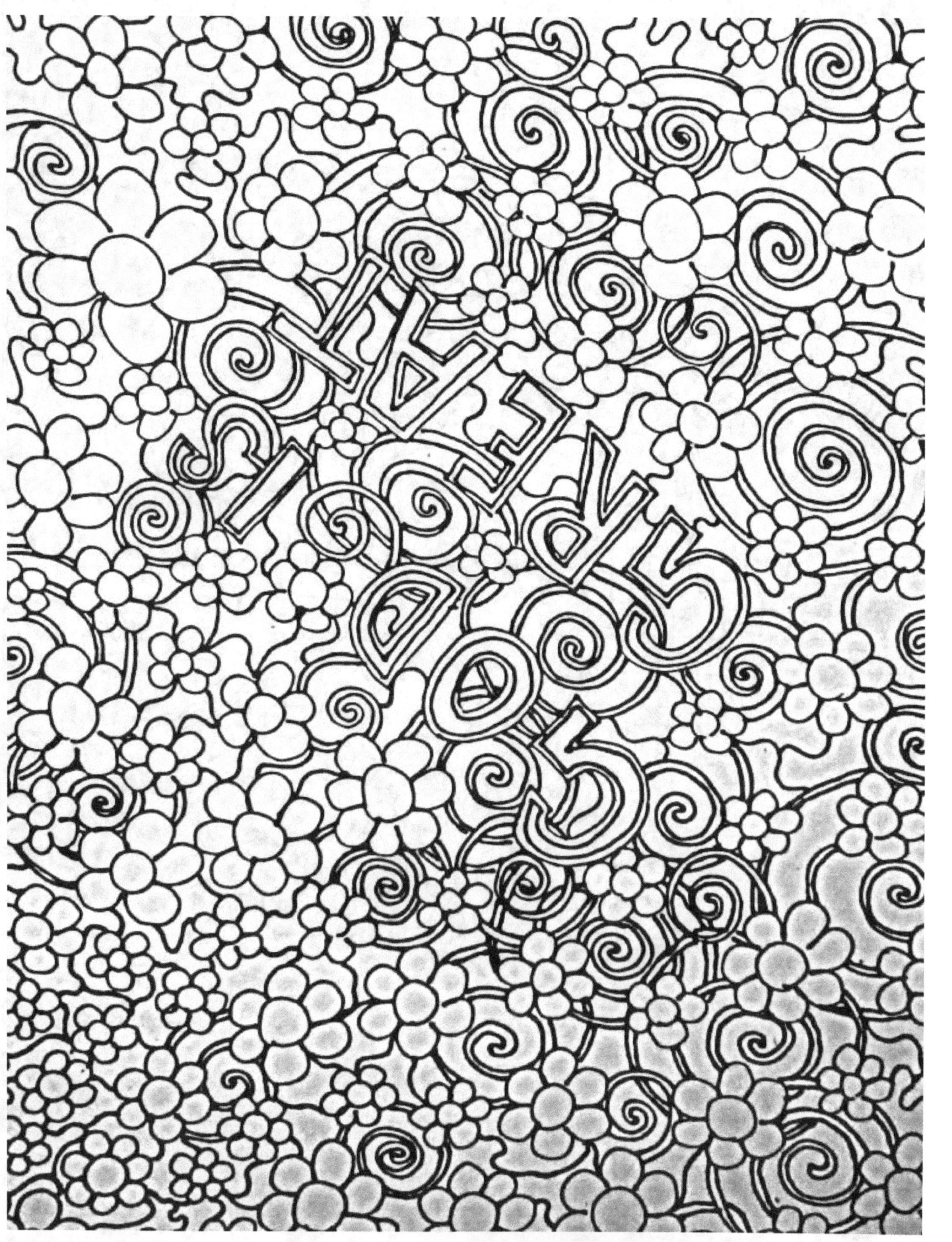

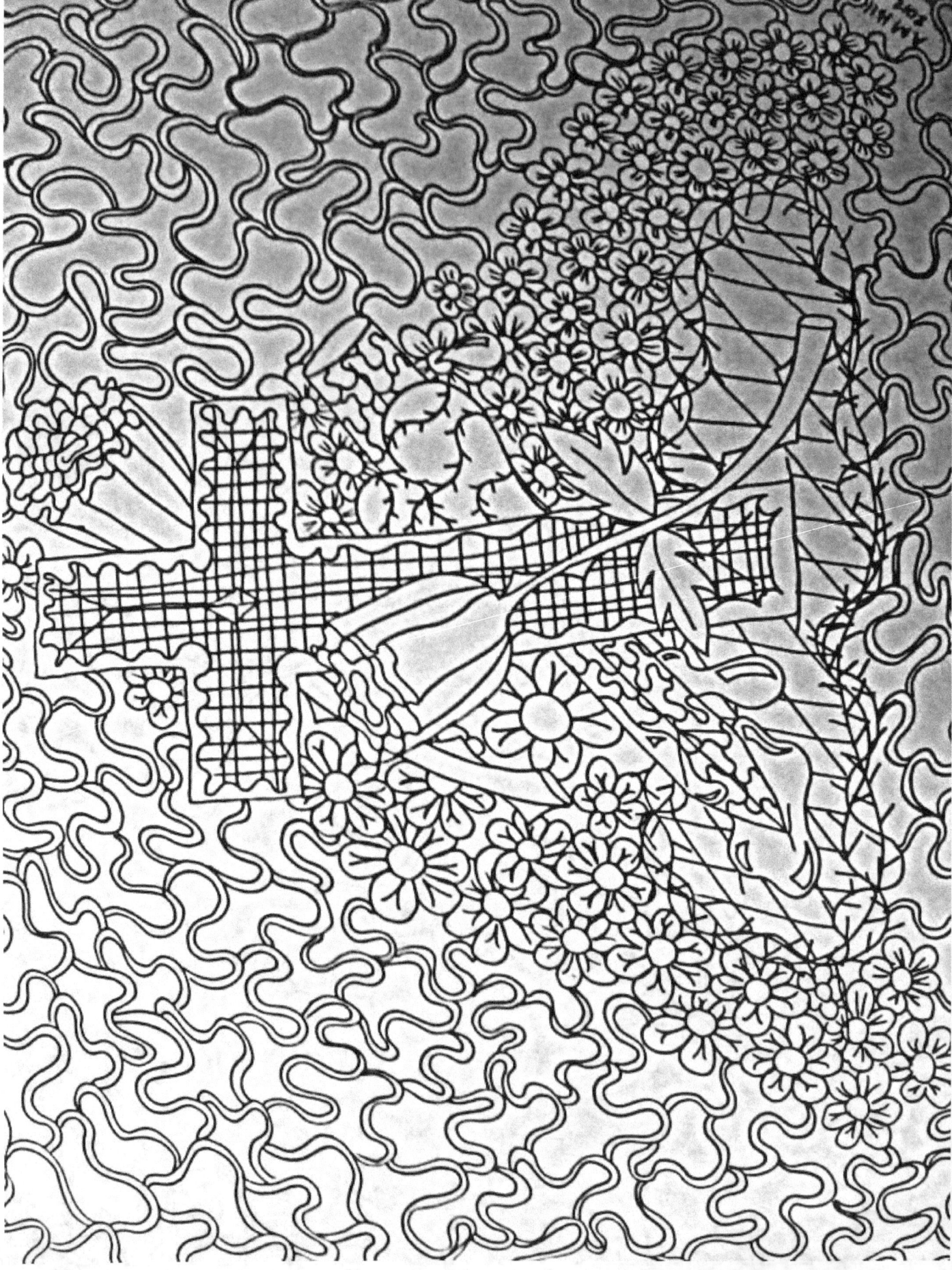

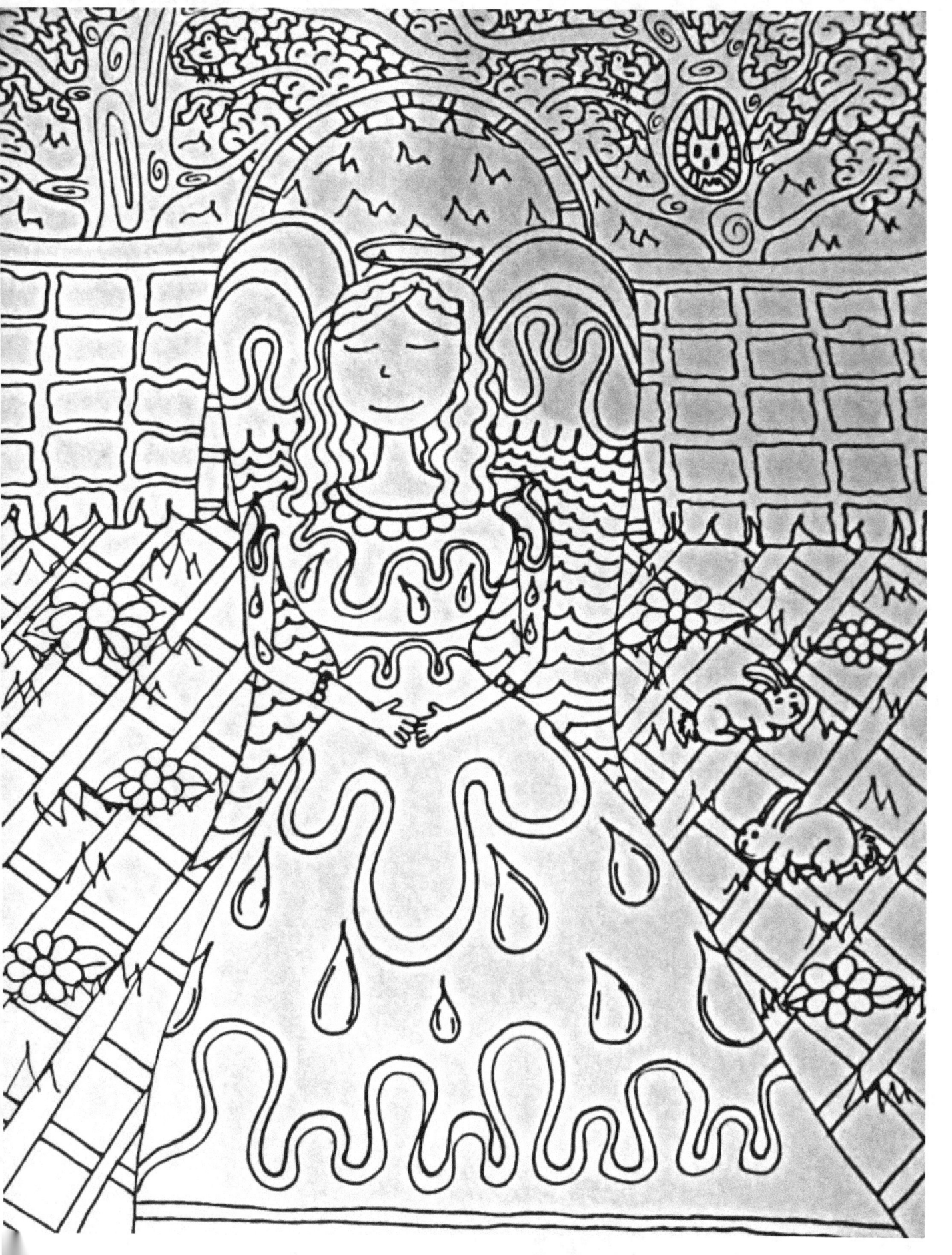